MARATHON
LEADERSHIP

26.2

Essential Lessons for Modern Leaders

DAVID D. KNAPP, Ph.D.

MARATHON
LEADERSHIP

For Kathy

"Cum amore in corde meo, corpore et anima...in aeternum"

Contents

PART THREE: RACING PRINCIPLES

PART FOUR: RECOVERING PRINCIPLES

Introduction

ONE MORNING SEVERAL YEARS AGO, I was struggling on a long training run. I was tired. It was cold and rainy. And I had a lot of other things I could have been doing back in my warm, dry office.

But I was in the midst of an intense training cycle for a marathon, where I hoped to set a PR (Personal Record). That meant that skipping or abbreviating my long run that cold, rainy day wasn't an option.

Hoping to distract myself, I started thinking about how my hobby had a lot in common with my profession (leadership training and coaching). It worked. Almost instantly, my feet felt lighter and the chilling rain more bearable as I contemplated this idea for the rest of my fifteen miles.

When I got home, I threw on dry clothes, headed to my office, and compiled a list of the leadership lessons I'd learned by training for and completing marathons. This initial list contained about a dozen lessons and included brief commentary on why learning and living the lessons was a requirement for anyone wanting to be a better leader—both runners and non-runners alike.

My list expanded over the years as participating in more marathons taught me more leadership lessons. Inevitably, it reached the magical number 26 (one lesson for each mile of a full marathon). When it did, I decided two things:

1. It was time to finalize the list by adding the .2 ("point to") being a leader, and

2. It was time to teach these lessons to the leaders I worked with.

The Purpose of This Book

I wrote *Marathon Leadership*: *The 26.2 Essential Lessons for Modern Leaders* to help you become a better leader—whether you're a marathoner, recreational runner, or self-avowed "couch potato" who doesn't like to *drive* 26.2 miles let alone *run* that distance. Now, those of you who are runners may pick up some training or racing tips along the way. But those tips are not the primary focus of this book. They're simply the byproduct of using the marathon as a metaphor for becoming a better leader.

And I believe that metaphor is appropriate for two reasons:

First, both running a marathon and becoming a better leader require you to undertake a deeply personal and transformational journey. Because I've taken those journeys and coached others during theirs, I know these 26.2 lessons will help you on your own leadership journey.

Second, a marathon symbolizes so much more than just a running event. For example, the word "marathon" is now used to describe any epic or heroic effort. Writers and broadcasters refer to "marathon battles," "marathon negotiations," and "marathon debates on the floor of the Senate." And over the years, countless products and even entire organizations (such as Marathon Oil) have included the word in their names to create the impression of endurance and durability.

These powerful associations with "marathon" are why I've dedicated my professional life to creating "marathon leaders." Becoming one involves ordinary people building the skills and endurance necessary to overcome the challenges facing their communities, businesses, and political organizations.

This is critical. For as I'll discuss in Lesson 1, the world's most challenging problems (global pandemics, climate change, and wealth inequality, for example) cannot be solved by management, which is a short-term sprint.

They will be overcome only through effective Marathon Leadership, which focuses on the long-term journey.

The Structure of This Book

To help guide you on your personal leadership journey, I've divided the 26.2 lessons into four sections, three of which are based on the natural stages of completing a marathon (training, racing, and recovering):

- *Part One (Lessons .2–6)*: General principles that leaders and marathoners, or leadership and marathons, have in common
- *Part Two (Lessons 7–15)*: What training to become a better leader has in common with training for a marathon
- *Part Three (Lessons 16–24)*: How to become a better leader by drawing on marathon racing tips
- *Part Four (Lessons 25–26)*: What leaders can learn from the often-overlooked, but critical, recovery phase of running a marathon

Because neither marathoners nor leaders have a lot of free time, I've kept the lessons short and to the point. Each one is approximately 500–1,500 words, which is the average length of most blog posts and magazine articles. My goal was to write an "airplane read"—a book packed with valuable information that was presented so succinctly it could be read from cover to cover during a typical domestic flight.

Don't let this brevity fool you, however. I promise that even the shortest lesson contains at least one key learning point that will help you on your leadership journey.

I also tried to keep the writing as relaxed and conversational as possible. In fact, I recommend you approach reading this book the same way I approached writing it. Whenever I wrote, I imagined the two of us in one of the following situations:

1. Sitting across from each other in the comfortable chairs at my local coffee shop, sipping our hot drinks on a cold winter day while talking about leadership; or

2. Stretched out in the finish area after a race, savoring an ice-cold beer on a hot summer day while talking about running.

By picturing us in one of these two informal settings as I wrote, I hope I've achieved the level of open and honest communication that is the hallmark of a good coach/coachee relationship.

But in the end, I can only help you so much. For just as no one else can run a marathon for you, no one else can make you a marathon leader. You must complete that journey yourself.

If so, I suggest you follow the advice of the Chinese philosopher Lao-Tzu, who wrote in the *Tao Te Ching* that "the journey of a thousand miles begins with a single step."[1] In this case, the journey to becoming a marathon leader begins with the turning of a single page ...

PART ONE:
General Principles

26.2

AS I RECORDED THE 26.2 LESSONS, I discovered that most of them could be categorized under the three natural stages of completing a marathon: training, racing, and recovering. But a few of the lessons were broader, more general characteristics that leaders and marathoners or leadership and marathons have in common. So, I placed these general principles first.

I believe the seven lessons in Part One are the most important (and often the most controversial) of the 26.2. At least that's what participants have told me in my Marathon Leadership® workshops. And I agree.

Why are they so important and so controversial?

For starters, I'll ask you in Lesson .2 to *honestly* examine your individual motives for wanting to be a leader. And then I'll politely, yet firmly, discourage some of you from ever becoming leaders if you're doing it for the wrong reasons.

Next, I'll slay a few of leadership-development's "sacred cows" in Lessons 1–3, including the outdated belief that leadership and management are the same; that great leaders are only made, not also born; and that organizations are machines that can be controlled by leaders.

In Lesson 4 I'll tackle a politically incorrect topic by arguing that modern leaders need to take better care of their bodies. Lesson 5 disputes the notion that drive and a highly results-oriented personality are always positive traits for leaders. Finally, Lesson 6 will reinforce how difficult it is to be a great leader. And even though the very challenge of it is what makes the leadership journey so rewarding, I'll remind you again that it's not for everyone.

I hope the seven lessons in Part One change some of your current beliefs about leadership. But even if they don't, they should at least challenge you to examine *why* you disagree with me. For as you'll learn in Lesson 9, there's no single "best" way to train leaders or marathoners, which means there's no single "best" way to think about leadership or marathons.

LESSON .2:

The "Point To" Being a
Leader Is Serving Others.

PRIOR TO THE 1908 LONDON OLYMPICS, marathons were a neat and tidy 25 miles long. But organizers decided to start this Games' race at Windsor Castle and end it at the White City Stadium in West London, which added a 26th mile to the course. Then, members of the royal family "suggested" (cough, cough) that the race finish beneath Queen Alexandria and other VIPs in the royal box. So, marathoners were required to run another 385 yards (.2 miles) on the cinder track after they entered the stadium.[2]

As unusual and random as it was, the 26.2-mile "English marathon" caught on and became the official marathon distance in 1924. Since then, every marathon has had a .2 added to it. Usually, the .2 is at the end of the race, after the mile 26 marker. However, some races reverse this by starting with the .2 and counting down the miles from the 26-mile marker. But whether it begins or ends the marathon, the .2 is the same.

That's not the case with the "point to" being a leader. If you don't start your leadership journey with the appropriate purpose of leadership guiding you, you'll never reach your ultimate destination of becoming a great leader. That's why leadership as service to others is the first lesson, not the last.

Servant-Leadership

Robert K. Greenleaf introduced "Servant-Leadership" in his seminal 1970 essay, *The Servant as Leader*,[3] after reading Herman Hesse's *Journey to the East*.[4] The novel focuses on a group of men engaged in a mythical journey that is sponsored by a secret Order. Traveling with these men is a servant named Leo, who takes care of all their menial chores. More importantly, Leo also entertains them with songs and lifts their spirits when they encounter difficulties along the way.

The journey is going well until Leo disappears. In his absence, things quickly fall apart, and the journey is abandoned.

Years later, the narrator (one of the travelers) is taken into the Order that sponsored the journey. Imagine his surprise when he discovers that Leo is the well-respected and well-loved leader of the Order. This plot twist led Greenleaf to conclude that not only are great leaders seen as servants first, *it is because they are servants first that they are seen as great leaders.* It was this powerful realization that inspired Greenleaf to pen his groundbreaking essay.

Both a broad leadership philosophy and specific set of leadership skills and practices, servant-leadership begins with a service-first perspective (as opposed to a leader-first mentality). Instead of initially focusing on gaining power, prestige, and material wealth, the servant-leader focuses first on sharing power, developing people, and meeting the needs of others. Consequently, servant-leaders see others as partners in a transformational process that develops both leader and followers—with the ultimate goal of creating more servant-leaders, who will repeat the process.

This does NOT mean servant-leaders don't value traditional organizational metrics, such as efficiency, growth, and profits. Nor does it mean they don't desire individual measures of success, such as financial rewards, increased responsibilities, and ego gratification. It simply means servant-leaders understand that the best way to get those results is by gaining the commitment of others.

Fifty years after their introduction, Greenleaf's ideas on servant-leadership are still influencing leaders and entire organizations around the world. But while Greenleaf's message remains as powerful as ever, his terminology hasn't aged as well. Many of the leaders I work with (especially young leaders) bristle at the word "servant." To keep them from getting sidetracked by the semantics of this powerful approach to leadership, I encourage them to use the term "service leadership" instead.

Please do the same if you don't like the word "servant." Because what we call this others-first approach to leadership matters far less than how effectively we execute it. And speaking of execution …

Now that I've introduced you to the philosophy of servant-leadership, let's examine the specific skill sets required to be an effective service-first leader.

The 10 Fundamental Skills of Servant-Leadership

Larry C. Spears (former president and CEO of The Greenleaf Center for Servant-Leadership) identified 10 fundamental skills of servant-leadership,[5] which I've summarized in **Figure 1** on page 4.

Nothing on this list should shock or scare you. These are not unrealistic, "touchy-feely" characteristics that have no application in the business world. They're basic communication and relationship skills that every leader (and, frankly, every human) should learn and live. Master these 10 critical skills, and your journey to becoming a better leader will be nearly complete. They're that important.

To illustrate how important, let me share the following example of servant-leadership in action.

Figure 1: The 10 Fundamental Skills of Servant-Leadership

1. *Listening:* Servant-leaders actively listen to others, including direct reports, and take their thoughts and opinions into consideration when making critical decisions. They also recognize that part of being a good listener is paying attention to what is *not* said, including nonverbal communication.

2. *Empathy:* Servant-leaders constantly try to empathize with others, even when they disagree with them. Treating others with respect and understanding helps servant-leaders better develop and meet the needs of the people around them.

3. *Healing:* Servant-leaders are good at healing themselves and others when dealing with issues surrounding doubt, conflict, problem-solving, and failure.

4. *Awareness:* Servant-leaders have high awareness of themselves and others, which allows them to view situations from an integrated, holistic perspective that includes ethics and values.

5. *Persuasion:* Servant-leaders focus on convincing for commitment, rather than on coercing for compliance.

6. *Conceptualization:* Servant-leaders focus beyond just day-to-day business transactions, never losing sight of long-term organizational goals and objectives. (In traditional management terminology, this is the difference between executing at the tactical level versus the strategic level.)

7. *Foresight:* Servant-leaders are like chess masters, able to visualize and anticipate future outcomes based on current actions. Closely related to conceptualization, foresight involves using past experiences and current realities to accurately identify future outcomes.

8. *Stewardship:* Servant-leaders hold their organization in trust for the greater good of society, which requires transparency, honesty, and integrity.

9. *Commitment to Growing People:* Servant-leaders nurture the personal, professional, and spiritual (emotional) growth of employees. This includes encouraging individuals to constantly strive for individual improvement, not just organizational profit.

10. *Building Community:* Servant-leaders strive to build a strong community within their organizations, and they make sure their organizations are positive contributors to their external communities.

A few years ago, I was working with a director in a Fortune 500 company when he was told to slash 10% of his departmental budget for the next fiscal year. He immediately recognized he could cut even more than the requested 10% by reducing staff. He also realized that doing so would demonstrate a commitment to cost savings and the bottom line, a mentality his organization greatly valued.

Before he made any final decisions, I asked him to ponder the "10 Fundamental Skills of Servant-Leadership" in depth. He had always considered himself a servant-leader, so he spent hours privately contemplating the 10 skills and discussing them with me in the context of the difficult situation he was facing.

After doing so, he concluded that the ONLY real benefactor of the reduction-in-staff approach would be him. Even the organization was going to suffer if he chose that action because his department was already understaffed. And cutting it further would damage customer service and satisfaction, perhaps beyond repair.

In the end, he met the budgetary goal without any reduction in force, even though it wasn't easy to find an "extra" 10% to cut. Both his executive team and direct reports (who watched colleagues being walked out of the building by their managers) appreciated his effort. And at the time of this book's publication, he's now a widely respected vice president in that same organization.

This is just one example of an individual being personally rewarded for exemplifying servant-leadership. I've witnessed countless others. Remember, service-first leadership does not mean you can't strive for and then enjoy the financial rewards, increased power, and ego gratification of being a successful leader. It simply means you should view those as the rewards of being a successful servant-leader, not the driving force behind your decisions and leadership actions.

And that leads me to a sensitive, but necessary, request.

If you cannot accept that leadership is about serving others, **PLEASE AVOID LEADERSHIP OPPORTUNITIES**. Doing so will spare your peers, your manager, your organization, your potential direct reports, and even yourself, a lot of pain and misery.

Because the unfortunate reality is that most organizations, including yours, already have enough individuals with leader-first mentalities in positions of power. What they desperately need instead are others-first leaders who are dedicated to learning and living the fundamental skills of servant-leadership.

LESSON 1:

Leadership Is a Marathon; Management Is a Series of Sprints.

MARATHONERS AND SPRINTERS ARE ALIKE in some ways. Both engage in the sport of running. Both share the same goals of improved individual performance and personal success. And both must train with discipline and focus to achieve these goals.

But that's where the similarities end.[6]

To finish a 26.2-mile race that will take even the world's best runners over two hours to complete, marathoners must build endurance, mental toughness, and aerobic capacity (the efficient use of oxygen as fuel). So their training focuses on logging high-mileage workouts week after week to develop their long, thin "slow-twitch" muscles.

Sprinters—whose races last seconds, not hours—must build speed, power, and anaerobic capacity (the efficient use of sugar as fuel). So they engage in high-intensity, low-mileage workouts to develop their short, thick "fast-twitch" muscles.

Over the years, I've come to view leadership versus management through the same prism as I use to examine marathons versus sprints. Leaders and managers both attempt to influence the behaviors of others. They both share the same goals of improved individual performance and organizational success. And both must work hard to develop their specific skill sets.

But like a marathoner thrust into a sprint or a sprinter forced to run a marathon, leaders and managers often find that their highly developed skills in one role do not translate into success in the other role. That's because the differences between leadership and management far outnumber their similarities. (See **Figure 2: The Leadership/Management Continuum**[7] on the next page.)

The Marathon Leader

Experienced marathoners know the real marathon begins around mile 20, when their minds, bodies, and spirits all are exhausted. But they still have another 6.2 miles to complete. Consequently, they're already thinking about and planning for the final 6.2 miles of the race when the starting gun sounds.

Like experienced marathoners, successful leaders know they can't lose sight of the future by focusing too heavily on the present. This mentality allows them to execute long-term visions, even when it might be easier to settle for short-term results.

Business lore is filled with examples of marathon leaders in action, but I've chosen the following two examples because both IBM and Apple are former clients. More importantly, they are great illustrations of Marathon Leadership in action.

IBM's System/390

When Lou Gerstner took over as IBM's CEO in April 1993, the company was in serious trouble.[8] Its stock was tanking. It was hemorrhaging cash. And its competitors were clobbering them in many key markets and lines of business.

Fortunately, their System/390 mainframe was generating substantial revenues and profits. Yet, the first major decision Gerstner made was to announce a significant price reduction plan for the S/390, one that would slash the very revenues and profits that were a lone bright spot in an otherwise dark and dismal financial landscape.

Why did he begin with such a risky and painful (at least in the short term) approach? Because he realized his competitors, particularly Hitachi and Fujitsu, were taking advantage of IBM's "milking" of their most successful products by pricing 30 to 40% less than them. And if IBM didn't absorb the short-term pain of dropping their prices to compete, their competitors would steal all of their key customers.

Figure 2: The Leadership/Management Continuum

LEADERSHIP	MANAGEMENT
• Is an informal role earned by one's personal power *with* people	• Is a formal role granted by one's position power *over* people
• Is an influence relationship between leader and follower	• Is an authority relationship between manager and direct report
• Is based on broad, subjective principles	• Is based on specific, objective goals
• Is difficult to measure and quantify (many "shades of gray")	• Is easy to measure and quantify (mostly "black and white")
• Emphasizes developing people	• Emphasizes executing tasks
• Strives for individual engagement and organizational effectiveness (transformational)	• Strives for individual execution and organizational efficiency (transactional)
• Relies on people and relationships	• Relies on processes and procedures

• Values creative thinking and subjective, intuitive decision-making	• Values critical thinking and objective, rational decision-making
• Rewards innovation, originality, and adaptability	• Rewards administration, replication, and stability
• Believes employees are valuable partners	• Believes employees are valuable resources
• **Focuses on long-term strategy and vision**	• **Focuses on short-term tactics and results**

When Gerstner announced his decision, it was met with harsh criticism, both internally and externally. But in the end, his focus on the long-term vision paid off. The price reduction helped IBM retain key customers long enough for it to develop a new-and-improved version of the S/390. This updated version was based on revolutionary technology and was so successful that it ultimately drove their largest competitor (Hitachi) out of the mainframe business altogether.

Apple's iPhone

Although Apple's iPod was dominating the music-player market in 2005, CEO Steve Jobs was distraught because he realized that a high-quality cell phone containing a well-designed music player could quickly render their hot product obsolete. This was not just irrational worry. Cell phones were already doing this very thing to digital cameras. And at the time, the iPod accounted for nearly 50% of Apple's revenue.[9]

Jobs realized that because everyone already carried a phone, Apple needed to get a quality product combining phone, music player, and camera to market as quickly as possible. Therefore, he put the iPad (which was already under development) on hold and transferred those resources to the iPhone.

His decision did not sit well with everyone at Apple. But looking back, no one can question Jobs's insistence that Apple throw all of its collective time, energy, and resources into the development of the iPhone. By staying focused on future opportunities, not on current successes, Jobs helped Apple make technological, marketing, and sales history.

These are just two examples of why leadership is a marathon, not a sprint. Like the marathoner who must focus on "the long run" (literally!), great leaders must develop, communicate, and successfully execute long-term visions for their organizations and employees. Failure to do so will lead to their demise.

But this doesn't mean that leadership is more important than management. On the contrary, marathon leaders cannot succeed without effective sprinter managers.

The Sprinter Manager

When I share "The Leadership/Management Continuum" in my leadership training sessions, participants often note that management isn't portrayed in a positive light. And they're right. Over the years, many authors have argued that management is inferior to leadership. I've even seen it referred to as "leadership's unsexy antithesis" and "a necessary evil in modern organizations." OUCH!

But the reality is that even great leaders will fail if they lack good managers to execute their long-term visions. Gerstner's decision to remain competitive in the mainframe market by slashing prices would have been a disaster if great managers at IBM hadn't been able to keep the updated S/390 project on track. And Jobs's vision for the industry-changing iPhone never would have been realized if successful managers at Apple hadn't been able to effectively execute that vision.

Like sprinters, managers *must* focus on short-term bursts of execution, using all the characteristics listed under the management column on page 9. In most organizations, especially if they're publicly held, these management sprints are quarterly: 90-day races that will be followed immediately by another 90-day sprint ... and another ... and another. And therein lies the danger of management's sprinter mentality—the consequences of which I'll discuss in Lesson 26.

A Final Thought

People often ask me if it's possible to be good at both leading and managing. The short answer is "absolutely." The longer answer is two-fold:

1. You need to accept that it's not easy to be good at both. This acceptance is an important first step in your leadership development, and
2. You must determine if (and subsequently how) you can be good at both. This involves a lengthy self-awareness and self-development process, one that includes the honest appraisal of your inherent personality, level of emotional intelligence, likes and dislikes, workplace experience, training, and a host of other variables.

In general, I believe each of us has a natural predisposition toward one side of the continuum, a somewhat controversial view I'll explore in Lesson 2. However, that doesn't mean we can't learn how to successfully display the skills on the other side of the continuum. It simply means it will take more effort. But as you'll learn in Lesson 6, accomplishing anything worthwhile always does.

LESSON 2:
Great Leaders, Like Great Marathoners, Are Both Born and Made.

A POPULAR SAYING IN THE MARATHON COMMUNITY is, "The first step to becoming a great marathoner is choosing your parents wisely." And while it's obviously tongue-in-cheek, it is true that at least part of a marathoner's potential success was determined at birth.

In a nutshell, some of us are born with a high percentage of slow-twitch muscle fibers and are naturally predisposed to sports that require long periods of aerobic endurance (distance running, long-course swimming, road cycling, etc.). Others are born with a high percentage of fast-twitch muscle fibers, predisposing them for success in sports that require high-intensity, but relatively short, periods of anaerobic activity (sprinting, basketball, weightlifting, etc.).[10]

But not having this genetic predisposition doesn't mean we can't become great marathoners. Runners often outperform more genetically gifted competitors by training harder and smarter. Therefore, the belief that great marathoners are both born for success **and** made through effective training methods is widely accepted in the running community.

Not so in the field of leadership development.

There, the expression, "Leaders are made, not born" is repeated over and over again as if it were a scientific law—despite the fact that most human-development experts now agree the old "nature versus nurture" argument is a false dichotomy. There's simply too much scientific evidence that *all* aspects of human development, including leadership, are influenced by both genetics and environmental factors.

Nature's Role in Developing Leaders

People who readily accept genetic predispositions for physical characteristics often find it much more difficult to accept genetic predispositions for mental, emotional, and behavioral characteristics. But once the human genome map was completed in 2003, it was only natural that researchers began looking for possible genetic links to leadership.

And it only took a decade for them to find one.

In 2013, a team of researchers led by Dr. Jan-Emmanuel De Neve announced that they had identified a "leadership gene" (genotype rs4950). De Neve's team made the discovery after analyzing DNA samples from approximately 4,000 individuals and then matching those samples to information about the test participants' jobs and relationships.[11]

This robust methodology, which included analyzing data from two large US health studies (The National Longitudinal Study of Adolescent Health and The Framingham Heart Study) made the team's findings powerful. By examining pairs of identical twins (who share the same genes) and non-identical twins (who share only half their genes but normally grow up in the same environment), the researchers were able to conclude that about 25% of the observed differences in leadership traits between participants could be explained by genetics alone.

These findings provided the first true genetic link to leadership success.

However, we need to add another inherited trait to these percentages: cognitive intelligence, or intelligence quotient (IQ).

Because IQ is one's *ability* to learn, not simply getting smarter through learning, some of it is fixed from birth as well. Granted, IQ is not a great predictor of success in any position (leadership or other), but research does indicate it accounts for approximately 5%–10% of one's success in any given role.[12]

Finally, one's personality (their overall style, preferences, or priorities—such as introversion versus extroversion) must be considered as well. Longitudinal studies have demonstrated that personality traits have some genetic component. But it's hard to quantify just how much, let alone how much those personality traits have on one's leadership success. However, both research and common sense tell us there is *some* level of influence that was determined at birth. Therefore, if we conservatively assign it the same percentage as that of IQ, we can conclude that at least 35%–45% of your success as a leader is determined by nature and is outside of your control.

Why Nature Versus Nurture Matters

It may seem that assigning a certain percentage of leadership ability to nature, not nurture, isn't a big deal. After all, even if 45% of your leadership potential was determined at birth, you'd still control over half of your potential success. Like the marathoner who didn't win the genetics lottery but finds success through smart, disciplined training, *you* control much of your success as a leader. It all comes down to how much effort you're willing to put into developing your leadership skills (the "nurture" component of leadership development).

Having said that, I believe the nature versus nurture argument is important in one critical area of your leadership journey: setting realistic expectations for success. Can anyone, including you, become a better leader? Absolutely.

But are some individuals just not cut out to be great leaders, no matter how much they try? My thirty-plus years of experience in this field has convinced me that the answer to that question is "yes." Not everyone can become a great leader, no matter how hard they work at it.

For me, it goes back to the slow-twitch versus fast-twitch muscle analogy. Like athletes who are predisposed to certain sports based on their muscle composition, certain individuals seem to be predisposed to become great leaders. Others are not. And it's both unrealistic and unfair to expect certain individuals to become great leaders when they have a ceiling on their abilities to be one.

I realize this is a controversial view, one that many in my profession vehemently disagree with. Again, I am not saying people can't get better at leadership. I'm simply arguing that not every person is capable of becoming a good (let alone great) leader.

If you're wondering about your own potential, I suggest you follow the advice I gave you back in Lesson 1 on leadership versus management. The first step is to engage in some honest self-reflection about your leadership potential, as well as ask for input from the people who know you best (both personally and professionally). Then use that self-reflection and feedback to set *realistic* leadership-development goals. Finally, work hard at learning how to leverage your leadership strengths, while compensating for your leadership weaknesses, to reach those goals and become the best possible leader *you* can become.

While all that time and effort will be difficult, it's still easier than choosing your parents wisely.

LESSON 3:

A Marathoner's Body Is a Living System, Not a Machine. So Are Organizations.

IN HIS BOOK *Run to Overcome*, elite US marathoner Meb Keflezighi recounts asking his daughter's preschool teacher to inform him if any of the kids in her class became sick in the days leading up to the 2009 New York City Marathon. Although the teacher assured Meb she would do so, Keflezighi and his wife decided to keep their daughter out of school for a few days before the race.

Then one of his *other* daughters came down with the sniffles. This prompted Meb to leave his family and crash with a runner friend to avoid becoming infected before the marathon, one he would win with a personal best of 2:09:15 (a blistering 4:56 per mile pace).[13]

Meb's story is a great example of a marathoner recognizing his body is a living system. It's not enough for marathoners just to train hard. They also must obsess about what they eat and drink, make sure they get enough sleep and muscle recovery, and yes, do their best to avoid sick people in the days and weeks leading up to a race.

But marathoners are not the only folks who need to think of themselves as part of a living system. Leaders at all levels of an organization must accept that they are leading in living systems, not managing machines.

What does that mean? And why is understanding the differences between managing machines and leading living systems important? I'm glad you asked.

Organizations as Machines

The widespread belief that organizations are machines humans must manage can be traced back to two of the greatest thinkers in Western science and philosophy: Sir Isaac Newton and Rene Descartes. Through their influential writings, these two intellectual giants helped create the Western worldview that the universe and everything in it is one giant machine. And because this machine is a closed system in the Newtonian/Cartesian world, humans can manipulate its parts however they see fit.

In the United States, this mechanistic worldview became the foundation of organizational structure and thought in the late nineteenth and early twentieth centuries, thanks to the work of Frederick Winslow Taylor.[14] Widely recognized as one of the world's first organizational/management consultants, Taylor was obsessed with organizational efficiency and productivity. This obsession was based on his belief that human workers literally were nothing more than interchangeable cogs in the machines of industry.

For example, one of his productivity improvement techniques involved using a stopwatch and tape measure to teach workers optimal performance mechanics. If they refused to work at that optimal pace (or simply couldn't maintain it), he fired them. Taylor also believed that the average factory worker "resemble[d] in his mental make-up the ox more than any other type," and repeatedly told workers, "I have you for your strength and mechanical ability. We have other men paid for thinking." YIKES!

While Taylor's beliefs about and attitude toward human workers were offensive, his methods and results were wildly successful. One hundred years after his death, he is still regarded as the father of scientific management theory and one of the most significant contributors to the success of the Industrial Revolution. His mechanistic techniques and practices were studied and replicated around the world, thereby cementing the "machine" mentality in human-created organizations.

More importantly, his views on how to manage organizations as machines were instilled in generations of leaders taught to believe their organizations were exempt from the systemic influences that maintain balance in every naturally occurring system on Earth. These leaders learned to manage their employees, teams, departments, and organizations as separate, interchangeable parts of a closed-system machine they could control and change at will. (See the left-side column of **Figure 3: Are You Managing a Machine or Leading in a Living System?** on page 20.)

Organizations as Living Systems

Fortunately, the organizations as machines paradigm is being relegated to the dustbin of history by a new paradigm: organizations as living systems. Based on the works of Donella Meadows, Peter Senge, Meg Wheatley, and countless other thought leaders, this new paradigm recognizes that individual humans and the organizations they create are open, self-organizing systems—not closed machines.[15] (See the right-side column of **Figure 3: Are You Managing a Machine or Leading in a Living System?**[16] on page 20.)

This philosophy further argues that human organizations should follow the example of nature, which is filled with self-organizing systems that rely on constant feedback loops to change or balance themselves, not on external control or manipulation. For example, if the rabbit population in an area dwindles, the number of foxes and coyotes will drop accordingly, because both predators rely on rabbits as a key food source. Conversely, an explosion in the rabbit population guarantees an increase in their predators' numbers.

Figure 3: Are You Managing a Machine or Leading in a Living System?

ORGANIZATION AS MACHINE	ORGANIZATION AS LIVING SYSTEM
Organizations are separate, interchangeable parts of a closed system (Newtonian based).	Organizations are interconnected relationships in an open system (Quantum based).
The goal is stability.	The goal is adaptability.
The emphasis is on individuals.	The emphasis is on the whole.
Managers engage in hierarchical command and control.	Leaders share responsibilities and partnerships.
Change is a "thing" that must be carefully controlled.	Change is a constant process that must be adapted to.
Objective reality exists and can be measured.	Reality is subjective, and all types of measurements are biased.
Employees are resources.	Employees are partners.
Critical thinking is valued.	Creative thinking is valued.
Rational, objective decision-making is emphasized.	Subjective, intuitive decision-making is emphasized.
Processes and procedures are static (laws).	Processes and procedures are dynamic (phases).
People earn a living by doing their individual jobs as part of producing organizational results.	People find meaning in their work, enriching their individual lives while producing organizational results.
The organization is a chart with boundaries, boxes, and reporting lines.	The organization is a web of relationships, processes, and information exchange.

Note that Mother Nature doesn't create a three-year strategic plan to increase predator and prey populations in a specific ecosystem. Nor does she replace the local ecosystem's alpha coyote with a younger hotshot from another ecosystem, challenging him to turn things around in terms of increased rabbit production.

Okay … okay … I'm being silly. But my point is serious. *Homo sapiens* is the only species (at least that we know of) that believes it is exempt from the systemic laws that govern every other species and naturally occurring system on the planet. And if we think we're exempt, we certainly believe our organizations are as well, which leads us to mistakenly manage our organizations as machines.

Shifting Paradigms: "The Five W's and H"

I could easily dedicate this entire book to the topic of shifting from managing a machine to leading in a living system. But I have 23 more lessons to cover, so I'll share just one deceptively simple tool to help you start thinking and leading more systemically: "The Five W's and H." (See **Figure 4** on page 22.)

"The Five W's and H" are a foundation of journalism, where articles must answer six basic questions: Who? What? When? Where? Why? and How? I simply adapted those questions into a systems-thinking template for the leaders I work with.

Each time you or your team members are contemplating a major decision or significant action, please ask "The Five W's and H" to gauge the impact of your decisions or actions on other parts of the organization. Keep in mind that this list is not meant to be exhaustive. Nor do I expect you to write down your answers each time you ask these questions. I'm simply encouraging you to stop and consider the overall systemic impact of your decisions and actions *prior* to making or taking them.

Figure 4: "The Five W's and H"

Whenever you or your team members are contemplating taking an action or making a far-reaching decision, take a few moments to answer the following questions as a proactive way of assessing the potential impact(s) on other parts of the organization:

- **Who** else will affected by this action?
- **Who** else should we proactively discuss this with?

- **What** information do we need to share with others?
- **What** are the possible implications of this action for others?

- **When** do we need to inform/involve others?
- **When** is it okay to move forward with this?

- **Where** could this action create problems for other parts of the organization?
- **Where** are our biases or narrow perspectives showing?

- **Why** do others need to know what we're doing?
- **Why** should we reconsider this action based on its overall impact?

- **How** will this affect other parts of the organization?
- **How should we communicate this to others (email, meeting …)?**

Incorporating "The Five W's and H" into your decision-making process will help you avoid spreading the serious infection of the machine mentality throughout your organization. But how do you know if it's already made your organization sick? That's easy. Just look for the following organizational illnesses: silos, a culture of mistrust, employee frustration, and (ironically) organizational inefficiencies. If you find evidence of these, the machine mentality has already spread.

And, believe me, those illnesses are lot more serious than the sniffles.

LESSON 4:

Marathoners and Leaders Need to Develop Both Their Minds and Their Bodies.

OVER THE PAST FEW DECADES, research on how much a runner's mind affects their performance during a marathon has exploded. The results of these studies are both consistent and stunning. Turns out, it's usually not your heart, lungs, or legs that cause you to slow down during a marathon. It's your brain.

For example, one study showed that putting false temperatures on thermometers participants could see while running, caused them to perform worse when they thought it was hotter than it actually was. And they performed better when they thought it was cooler than it actually was. Their bodies weren't reacting to true temperatures. Their brains were responding to false ones.[17]

Another study fed false competitor pacing data to participants. When participants believed their competitors were going faster than they truly were, their brains gave up and they slowed down—*even when they were capable of maintaining the actual pace of their competitors.* And you guessed it. When participants thought their competitors were moving slower than they actually were, they sped up and maintained a faster pace than what their physical conditioning should have allowed.

The bottom line is that mental training is just as important to marathon success as is physical training. Granted, all the mental training in the world won't get you through a marathon if you haven't put in the training miles. But focusing on JUST the physical is a recipe for disaster.

Unfortunately, too many leaders suffer from the exact opposite problem. They spend all their time developing their minds and forget about taking care of their bodies. And research shows that long-term inattention to their health eventually affects their performance as leaders. In fact, some studies indicate physical health and energy is a key differentiator between successful and unsuccessful leaders.

Exercise, Physical Health, and Leadership

Sharon L. McDowell-Larsen and her colleagues at the Center for Creative Leadership in Colorado Springs, Colorado, studied over 600 senior-level executives who attended a five-day leadership course at the Center. These researchers collected numerous sets of data concerning the executives' physical health and exercise levels, and then compared them to how others rated the executives as leaders. Their findings? There was a direct positive correlation between the participants' overall health and fitness levels and their perceived leadership abilities.[18]

This study is not an outlier.[19] The research linking physical fitness to improved performance at ALL levels of an organization is both voluminous and consistent. It was a foundation of Jim Loehr and Tony Schwartz's bestseller, *The Power of Full Engagement,* and is a driving force behind Schwartz's organization, The Energy Project˚. Other well-known leadership- and executive-training organizations, such as the Johnson & Johnson Human Performance Institute˚ and the Cooper Institute˚, also stress this mind/body connection in the workplace.[20] Heck, one study even showed an increase in a company's market value if its CEO was a marathoner![21]

This connection between physical fitness and success as a leader should come as no surprise. Most leadership positions require long hours, intense workweeks (often including weekends), and at least some travel if your organization is even moderate in size. And the higher one climbs the leadership ladder, the more these demands increase.

Therefore, individuals who take care of their bodies will be better equipped to deal with these physical demands in the long run (pun intended). In fact, Bob Johansen, Distinguished Fellow with the Institute for the Future, predicts in his book *Leaders Make the Future* that the best leaders will be the healthiest leaders. He further suggests that leaders who eat, drink, and travel too much, while exercising too little, will become less and less common in the organizations of the future.[22]

What This Means for Your Leadership Journey

Look, you don't have to be a great athlete to be a great leader. But if you're like most individuals (especially in the United States, where obesity is an epidemic), you *do* need to take better care of your body. That includes consistently engaging in the following behaviors, all of which will help you become and stay a better leader:

- Eating a healthy diet
- Maintaining an appropriate weight for your body's frame
- Engaging in some type of regular exercise or physical activity
- Stopping (or never starting) the use of tobacco products
- Limiting your intake of alcohol and recreational drugs
- Getting plenty of sleep
- Scheduling regular dental and medical checkups, including preventive tests and procedures.

While all leaders should practice these behaviors, only you can decide what works best for you and your body. Because like your individual approach to leadership development, which I'll discuss in Lesson 9, the magic formula for your physical health will be different from the magic formula for everyone else. That means you'll need to consult with your doctor, dentist, and other health care providers to discover yours.

But discover it, you must.

For as the Buddha wisely observed thousands of years before scientific research confirmed the body–mind connection: "To keep the body in good health is a duty ... otherwise we shall not be able to keep the mind strong and clear."[23] Nor will we have the strength, energy, and endurance to become a successful marathon leader.

LESSON 5:

Marathoners and Leaders Tend to Be Highly Driven, Results-Oriented Individuals. That's Not Always a Good Thing.

UNETHICAL RUNNERS HAVE CHEATED in marathons literally since the event's inception. During the inaugural marathon at the 1896 Olympics in Athens, local runner Spiridon Belokos finished in third place. But race officials later disqualified him after discovering he had ridden a number of late miles in a carriage and jumped out a few miles from the finish.[24]

This form of cheating is called "course cutting" or "pulling a Rosie," which is a reference to the most infamous course cutter in history: Rosie Ruiz at the 1980 Boston Marathon. Originally declared the female winner in a time of 2:31:56, Ruiz fell under immediate suspicion when race officials noticed she didn't look tired after running what, at that time, was the third-fastest women's time in Boston history. Also, she couldn't answer basic post-race questions from reporters about her approach to training and running the race. After an eight-day investigation, race officials disqualified Ruiz, concluding she had jumped on the course about a half mile from the finish.

Course cutting is not the only form of marathon cheating. Bib swapping (giving your race bib to a faster runner to record a faster time) and doping (using performance-enhancing drugs) have become far too widespread in the sport.

Even ethical runners engage in counterproductive behaviors. Burnout, eating disorders, and overtraining injuries are common in a sport filled with driven, results-oriented individuals.

Like their marathon brothers and sisters, many leaders fall victim to their own drive and results-oriented natures. Almost daily, we read or hear about some business or political leader getting caught engaging in unethical or illegal behaviors. And burnout among leaders is so common that I'll explore the topic in more depth in later lessons.

Your Leadership Credo

These stories of personal failings are why I encourage the leaders I work with to create leadership credos.[25] From the Latin *credos*, these are simple statements of a leader's core beliefs and values that drive their actions. Your leadership credo defines your character, serves as a moral compass to guide your behaviors on a daily basis, and helps others understand how you approach leadership.

To develop your personal leadership credo, begin by completing the following four self-reflective statements:

1. I gained my core beliefs about leadership from …
2. The two or three values that MOST define me as a leader are …
3. The people who work for me can always count on me to …
4. I am passionate about being a leader because …

Once you've explored these self-reflections, begin to wordsmith your credo. As you do, consider the following guidelines:

- *Be personal:* Speak in the first person.
- *Be open:* Let people know who you really are.
- *Be genuine:* Say what you actually believe.
- *Be brief:* Keep it short and simple.
- *Be courageous:* Put a stake in the ground.

Keep in mind there's really no right or wrong leadership credo format. It simply has to resonate with you, be brief enough to articulate quickly, and be easily understood by others. For example, here is my leadership credo: *"I create marathon leaders, who will make the world a better place."*

Notice that my credo is a complete sentence that reads like a personal vision or mission statement. Other leaders take different approaches, as you can see in the credos in **Figure 5**[26] on page 30. These examples, which I've collected over the years from leaders I've worked with, should help you create your unique leadership credo.

But simply creating and sharing your leadership credo isn't enough. You also must live it. And as Hamlet so wisely observed, "Aye, there's the rub."[27] Because no matter how much you may believe in your credo, you'll undoubtedly face numerous situations throughout your leadership career that will challenge you to follow through with it in your behaviors.

While it won't always be easy, you must stick to your core leadership beliefs and subsequent behaviors. After all, you don't want folks one day accusing some disgraced leader of "pulling a [insert *your* name]."

Figure 5: Sample Leadership Credos

"Everything with integrity."

"Be the best you can be."

"Strive for continuous improvement, growth, and learning."

"Be a servant-leader who creates other servant-leaders."

"I see the possibilities in everyone."

"Live the truth."

"Say what you do—do what you say."

"Family … Community … Country … God."

"Integrity. Adaptability. Encouragement."

"Show people you care for them."

"Internal cooperation—external competition."

"A diverse workforce is a strong workforce."

"Leadership by example."

"Never ask someone to do something you wouldn't do yourself."

"Treat others as *you* would like to be treated (The Golden Rule) AND treat others as *they* would like to be treated (The Platinum Rule)."

"Do your job."

"My goal is to develop leaders at all levels of the organization."

"Visibility and Accessibility."

"Honesty above all else."

"Caring. Sharing. Preparing."

LESSON 6:

If It Were Easy, Anyone Could Do It. But Then It Wouldn't Mean As Much.

WHEN MY WIFE AND I FIRST STARTED DATING, she wasn't a runner. In fact, she hated running. So I was pleasantly surprised when she accepted my invitation to travel with me to Oklahoma City, where I was going to complete the "Run to Remember" Memorial Marathon.

While I was out on the course that beautiful spring morning, Kathy hung out by the finish line. And that experience changed her life.

As she watched runners cross the finish line, she noticed some were dancing and laughing, many were crying, and everyone was spent but euphoric at their accomplishment. And she realized that maybe there was more to running (specifically running a marathon) than she had ever suspected. A few days after the race, she cautiously asked if I would put together a beginner running program for her with the possibility, however slight at that point, that she might want to run a marathon one day.

Fast-forward to the present ...

Kathy has not only run marathons, but she is now an Ironman˚ triathlete, having discovered she loves the variety of that sport. For those of you unfamiliar with triathlons, it combines swimming, biking, and running in a single event. And the Ironman˚ distance is one serious challenge—a 2.4-mile swim, 112-mile bike ride, and THEN a full marathon! As of this book's publication, she is training hard to earn a coveted age-group qualifier spot at the World Championships in Kona, Hawaii. And I have no doubt she'll accomplish that lofty goal someday.

But none of that would have happened if Kathy hadn't spent those hours watching marathoners cross the finish line in Oklahoma City. While doing so, she witnessed the tremendous sense of satisfaction that humans feel when they accomplish something challenging. For as Theodore Roosevelt once noted, "Nothing in the world is worth having or worth doing unless it means effort, pain, difficulty."[28] While TR wasn't specifically talking about completing a marathon or being a great leader, his thought applies to both activities.

For example, it is estimated that less than 0.5% of the US population, and well under 0.1% of the world's population, will ever complete a marathon. That's a fairly exclusive club. So, pushing oneself through all that "effort, pain, difficulty" to finish a marathon and join that club means a lot.

Unfortunately, being an effective—let alone great—leader is almost as exclusive a club.

It's difficult to determine exactly how many great leaders there are in our organizations because it requires measuring quality, not just quantity. But that doesn't mean researchers haven't tried. And their results range from the disappointing (approximately one-third of all organizational leaders are effective) to the truly frightening (only 8% of all organizational leaders are effective).

Regardless of what the actual percentage is, one thing is certain: being a great leader isn't easy. If it were, our organizations would be filled with them. And they're definitely not:

- A 2015 study conducted by Brandon Hall found that over 70% of the surveyed organizations did not believe their leaders would be able to lead their organizations into the future.[29]
- In a 2018 Development Dimensions International survey, only 41% of current organizational leaders and 37% of HR professionals believed the overall quality of their organizations' leaders was high.[30]

Why is being a great leader so incredibly difficult? I've asked that question to countless leaders over the years, and what follows are the top five reasons they've given me.

Why Leadership Is So Difficult

1. *Ego:* As you learned earlier, the entire "point to" being a leader is serving others. That means letting go of your ego to selflessly focus on the development and success of others. And that's something most leaders struggle with. But just because it's difficult doesn't mean it isn't a worthwhile goal. As was the case with the topic of leading in a living system, I could dedicate this entire book to how leaders can best overcome their egos to focus on others. Fortunately, I don't have to because someone else has already written a wonderful book on the topic: *Ego is the Enemy,* by Ryan Holiday.[31] I recommend this gem to every leader. Get it. Read it. Live it. You won't regret it.

2. *The Complexity and Imperfection of Human Beings:* I work with a lot of technical and scientific leaders, and almost every last one of them bemoans the challenges their fellow *homo sapiens* present—especially in comparison to the technologies and carefully controlled experiments with which they usually interact. Human beings are incredibly complex and imperfect creatures. When you combine them into teams, departments, and organizations, those complexities and imperfections increase exponentially. And it's up to the leaders

of those teams, departments, and organizations to deal with that exponential increase. Kind of makes running a marathon seem easy by comparison, huh?

3. *Accountability Without Responsibility:* Leaders are accountable for their team members' performance, whether it is a small project team or a large multinational corporation. But unlike when they were individual contributors, leaders are not personally responsible for that performance. They have to figure out how to motivate their team members to perform, instead of just worrying about their own performance. And that often involves a steep learning curve for those used to worrying only about themselves, which leads them right back to the above ego challenge.

4. *Lack of Training:* Too often, organizations give people leadership responsibilities without providing the coaching and training those individuals will need to succeed in these roles. As one leader I worked with put it, "It's not even like being thrown in the pool for the first time and told to 'sink or swim.' It's like being thrown in the pool for the first time and told 'you better win the gold medal in an Olympic swimming event.'" Being a leader requires very different skill sets than being a successful individual contributor, but organizations too often expect their leaders to be just as successful as they were as individual contributors, without having set them up for that success.

5. *Pace of Work/Lack of Time:* Though I listed this last, it's probably the one I've heard the most over the past few years ... and that was *before* the COVID-19 pandemic turned our world upside down. The pace of our lives, especially our professional lives, continues to speed up. But there are only so many hours in a day for leaders to accomplish everything they need to. This leads to tremendous pressure and stress on even the most organized and experienced leaders, let alone new leaders who are barely treading that water I alluded to above. That's

why Lesson 18 on knowing when to set the pace for others and when to let them set the pace will be an important leadership lesson.

These challenges, along with myriad others I didn't mention, make being a great leader difficult. But they also make it extremely rewarding for those individuals who face and successfully overcome those challenges.

So, if completing a marathon is something you have absolutely zero interest in doing, I suggest taking Roosevelt's advice and putting all that "effort, pain, difficulty" into becoming a great leader. Because there is no leadership "hack" that will make it easy for you (regardless of what self-proclaimed leadership gurus may promote on their podcasts, YouTube videos, or social-media memes).

But as my lovely bride can attest, sometimes those things in life that most challenge, intimidate, or, frankly, scare the living crap out of you, become the very things that provide the most meaning, joy, and sense of accomplishment.[32]

Part Two:
Training Principles

AS YOU LEARNED BACK IN LESSON 2, even the most naturally gifted runners or leaders still must develop those gifts through training if they hope to become great marathoners or leaders. The nine lessons in Part Two examine what training to become a better leader has in common with training to become a better marathoner.

Specifically, Lessons 7 and 8 will help you set realistic SMART or CLEAR goals and stretch goals. Lesson 9 emphasizes the importance of following the individual leadership-development path that's right for *you*, no one else. And while you'll have to traverse that leadership-development journey *for* yourself, you don't have to take it *by* yourself. That's why Lesson 10 provides tips for choosing the right leadership coach or mentor to help guide you along the way.

In Lesson 11, I'll discuss the importance of personal power and its tremendous impact on your leadership success. And because personal power includes the presence you project to others, Lesson 12 provides tips, techniques, and reminders for effective emotional self-awareness and expression.

Lesson 13 examines *association* and *disassociation*, because great leaders know when to focus and when to let go. In Lesson 14, I'll introduce you to a running legend—a soft-spoken Texas rancher who will remind you to "keep it simple" when you start overcomplicating things. Finally, Lesson 15 wraps up Part Two by focusing on the important leadership skill of active listening.

LESSON 7:
If Your Goal Is Unrealistic, You Will Fail. But ...

AS IS THE CASE WITH MANY ASPECTS OF TRAINING for and completing a marathon, accurately predicting finishing times based on a runner's pace at shorter distances has improved a lot over the past few decades. For example, a runner who completes a 10k race (6.2 miles) in 43:54 (a 7:03 pace) should be able to complete a full marathon in around 3 hours and 25 minutes (a 7:48 pace).[33]

This ability to accurately predict finish times is a godsend for novice runners, who tend to set unrealistic time goals for their first marathon. Based on those unrealistic time goals, these first-timers go out *way* too fast, practically guaranteeing a spectacular crash and burn over the second half-marathon. So setting a realistic pacing goal based on one's current fitness levels and sticking to it on race day is critical.

Unfortunately, leaders often make the same mistake. By setting unrealistic goals for their individual contributors, teams, departments, or entire organizations, they not only guarantee failure, they also create significant morale problems. Their people simply give up once they realize they'll never reach these unrealistic goals.

That's why following some type of goal-setting methodology is so important. And while there are numerous approaches to goal setting, the SMART methodology is undoubtedly the most widely recognized.

SMART Goals

SMART goals were first introduced by George T. Doran in a 1981 article in *Management Review*.[34] But the concept really took off when it became a foundation of legendary management guru Peter Drucker's "Management by Objectives" (MBO) methodology.[35]

SMART is an acronym that stands for **Specific, Measurable, Attainable, Relevant,** and **Time-bound**:

S   *Specific:* Effective goals are stated as concisely and explicitly as possible.

M   *Measurable:* Effective goals include Key Performance Indicators (KPIs) that can be measured for success or failure.

A   *Attainable:* Effective goals should be realistic, given the current situation (including time and resources). That doesn't mean they can't be challenging goals. They just need to be realistically achievable.

R   *Relevant:* Effective goals should make a difference, helping you achieve your individual, departmental, and organizational vision or mission.

T   *Time-bound:* Effective goals include a realistic time frame for completion.

Be aware that you might see different words used in the acronym: "Achievable" instead of "Attainable" or "Timely" instead of "Time-bound," for example. The semantics of the acronym aren't important. The execution of the format is. Because research shows that using the SMART format will force you to define and focus your goals in a way that makes it much more likely you'll achieve them.

Figure 6 below features SMART goals I've helped clients create over the years. Use these examples as a guide for generating your own SMART goals.

CLEAR Goals

The SMART goals methodology is a great tool. However, it has recently been criticized for being too rigid and unable to keep pace with today's lightning-fast, agile business environment. To combat this, Adam Kreek, a gold-medalist rower for Canada at the 2008 Beijing Olympic Games and a motivational speaker, created the CLEAR methodology of setting goals.[36]

Figure 6: Examples of SMART Goals

NOT SMART	SMART
"I will improve my sales closing rate."	"I will increase my sales closing rate to 10 service packages a month by year end."
"Our department will reduce the cost of poor quality."	"Our department will reduce the cost of poor quality in Q4 by 15% compared to Q1."

"We will improve our branch's customer service."	"We will improve our branch's customer satisfaction score from 7.2 to 8.0 by the end of Q2 through increased teller coverage during traditionally heavy traffic times (11:00 a.m. to 1:00 p.m. and 4:00 to 6:00 p.m.)."
"I will spend more time with my direct reports."	"I will meet one-on-one for 30 minutes with each of my direct reports weekly throughout the year."
"I will improve my leadership skills."	"I will complete two online and attend two classroom leadership trainings by the end of Q3."
"I will provide administrative support for my department."	"I will work with recruiting to post an admin. position by the end of the month and hire a qualified candidate for it by the end of the quarter."

Like SMART, CLEAR is an acronym, which stands for **Collaborative, Limited, Emotional, Appreciable,** and **Refinable**:

C   *Collaborative:* Goals should encourage employees to work together collaboratively and in teams.

L   *Limited:* Goals should be limited in both scope and duration.

E   *Emotional:* Goals should make an emotional connection to employees, tapping into their energy and passion.

A   *Appreciable:* Goals should be broken down into smaller goals, so they can be accomplished more quickly and easily for long-term gain.

R   *Refinable:* Goals should be set with a headstrong and steadfast objective. But as new situations or information arise, give yourself permission to refine and modify your goals.

To help you create CLEAR goals, Kreek recommends asking yourself 25 open-ended questions, which I've included in **Figure 7** below.

Ultimately, it doesn't matter which goal-setting format you use. Just make sure you create goals that are either SMART or CLEAR. Otherwise, you're inviting failure ... and that's just DUMB.

Figure 7: 25 Questions to Help You Create CLEAR Goals

Collaborative

- With whom should I work on this goal?
- Why do these collaborators matter?
- Who are we serving with this goal?
- What expertise do we need to achieve this goal?
- Who are the stakeholders for this goal? Employees? Customers? Shareholders?

Limited

- When do we start working on the goal?
- When do we stop working on the goal?
- Is this goal realistic?
- How will I know when the goal is met?
- What type of scope creep could develop?

Emotional

- What is the purpose of this goal?
- How will achieving this goal make a difference to us and the stakeholders?
- Do we *want* to do this? Or do we *have* to do this?
- Are we 100% committed to achieving this goal?
- Will achieving this goal lead to positive emotions for us and the stakeholders?

Appreciable

- What is the next, smallest, most-obvious action to help achieve this goal?
- What key performance indicators can I use for metrics?
- What key milestones exist in the achievement of this goal?
- What other goals will be accomplished on the road to accomplishing this goal?
- What objectives can I stack and track?

Refinable

- When will I revisit this goal to tweak it?
- What events (beyond my control) could require us to change this goal?
- What new information could require us to change this goal?
- What is most likely to go wrong?
- How will we adapt to the best-case scenario? Worst-case scenario? Most likely scenario?

LESSON 8:

... If You Stay in Your Comfort Zone, You'll Never Improve.

WHILE SMART GOALS ARE CRITICAL for achieving initial success, the fundamental principles of ANY physical-fitness training (including a marathon) are overload and recovery. Runners eventually must push their bodies beyond their comfort zones to build the muscular and aerobic endurance to finish a 26.2-mile race. This requires them to regularly reassess their fitness levels and design and execute workouts that force their bodies to work harder than they did at lesser fitness levels.

Of course, they must also make sure they don't push their bodies TOO far outside their comfort zones by not incorporating enough rest and recovery into their training (a topic I'll discuss in more detail in Lesson 26). To find this delicate balance, marathoners and their coaches create "stretch" workouts, which force runners out of their comfort zones while still maintaining achievable results.

Leaders also need to guard against staying in their comfort zones if they want to become better. To do so, they need to create "stretch" goals.

Stretch Goals

Stretch goals go beyond current capabilities and performance.[37] They also require a novel way of approaching a challenge. In other words, stretch goals are not just about working harder. Instead, they are about reaching a new level of performance through previously untapped skill sets and approaches. By design, stretch goals should take you outside of your comfort zone and can be an important part of your development process, especially if you're actively seeking a promotion.

But you have to be careful when setting stretch goals because they often are right on the edge of being unrealistic … the very thing I cautioned you about in Lesson 7.[38] The key is to follow these five guidelines for setting stretch goals:

1. *Make sure you or the person you're setting the stretch goals for are currently performing at a high level.* This should be a blinding flash of the obvious, but I regularly encounter leaders who set stretch goals for themselves or others when they or those they work with are not even meeting the current performance expectations. This is like a marathoner or their coach designing tougher workouts (faster pace, increased mileage, less recovery …) when they or their runner aren't even achieving the desired goals of their current workouts. Um, that's not a stretch goal … it's a pipe dream.

2. *Make sure the resources are in place to support the stretch goal.* If you don't have the time, money, or other resources to tackle a stretch goal with a reasonable chance of success, take the advice of Johnny Depp in the 1997 crime drama *Donnie Brasco* and "fuhgeddaboudit!" Seriously, setting a stretch goal without the resources to support it guarantees failure and the inevitable frustration, anger, drop in morale, etc. caused by that failure.

3. *Make sure you limit the number of stretch goals for yourself and others.* In general, I urge people to limit themselves or their team members

to one stretch goal at a time. Again, this should be intuitive, but given the driven nature I discussed in Lesson 5, people too often try to achieve multiple stretch goals simultaneously, once again guaranteeing failure of at least some of them.

4. *Make sure you allow for mistakes, and don't punish failure.* By their definition, stretch goals are difficult to achieve. I mean, if there's little chance for failure, it's not a stretch goal. So, you need to approach them with the understanding that failure is not only possible, it may very well be probable. This doesn't mean you should accept poor effort or sloppy execution. It simply means you need to prepare yourself for failure, no matter how hard you try to achieve the stretch goal.

5. *Make sure your stretch goals still adhere to the SMART or CLEAR formulas.* Just because a goal is a stretch, it isn't exempt from being Specific, Measurable, Attainable, Relevant, and Time-bound—or Collaborative, Limited, Emotional, Appreciable, and Refinable. On the contrary, I think it's even more important that stretch goals adhere to one of these goal-setting structures. Otherwise, you're back to creating pipe dreams, not stretch goals.

A Final Thought

You will need to find the balance between Lessons 7 and 8 if you want to become a better leader. Yes, the goals you set for yourself and others need to be realistic and attainable, but they also need to challenge you. I can't tell you exactly what that balance will be because it will be different for every goal, individual, and situation (the "magic formula" concept I'll introduce to you in Lesson 9).

But I CAN assure you of two things:

1. This balance between realistic, attainable goals and stretch goals does exist; and
2. Finding that balance will be worth it.

LESSON 9:

There Is No Single "Best" Way to Train Marathoners or Leaders.

AT THE END OF LESSON 8, I promised to introduce you to the "magic formula" concept. This simple, yet profound, notion was first identified by 2:13:00 marathoner Keith Dowling in one of my favorite marathon training quotes: "There is a magic formula ... it's just that the magic is different for everyone."[39]

For example, many marathoners swear by the high-mileage, periodization approach to training. Others find success through low-mileage, high-intensity programs. Some runners focus solely on running. Others incorporate cross-training workouts into their training regimen (cycling, swimming, yoga, etc.). The key is to identify the training approach that creates your own individual magic.

That's also the case with your leadership development. What works for others may not work for you. You need to identify and follow the approach that works best for you. But that doesn't mean there aren't some tried-and-true general steps to take. I'll introduce you to four of them in this lesson.

Nurturing Your Leadership Development

The first step in your leadership development is *identifying what type of learning works best for you*. If you prefer and can make time for traditional classroom training sessions, you should begin by signing up for those offered by your organization. If those courses are limited or even nonexistent (as is the case in many small organizations or start-ups), look for public sessions offered by vendors in your area.

For example, I'm based in the Denver, Colorado, area, and have a partnership with the Denver Training Group, through which I offer public sessions. And in keeping with the spirit of Lesson 19 (Competitors Are Wonderful Gifts), another organization called the Employer's Council® offers numerous public sessions in leadership throughout the Rocky Mountain region. I also recommend the Center for Creative Leadership, which offers many terrific leadership courses to the general public.[40]

If you enjoy classroom settings but are also looking for a certificate or degree, formal classes at a college or university may be the way to go. One word of caution, however. Carefully research the programs you're considering to make sure they approach their leadership courses from an applied perspective. As a former college and university instructor, I can attest that some traditional programs are so theoretical that they are basically useless for modern professionals looking to learn and apply practical skills.

If you prefer online learning, your options are more plentiful. Even before the COVID-19 pandemic, most colleges and universities offered online courses, with a number of institutions operating solely as online programs. And if you're not looking for a certificate or degree, you can choose from thousands of online training courses or webinars, many of which are free.

For those of you who enjoy self-paced, more informal learning opportunities, I highly recommend a subscription to the *Harvard Business Review*.[41] This publication is filled with valuable research and opinion pieces on all aspects of organizations, including leadership. (Many libraries carry it, so check your local branch to see if you can access it through a library membership.)

Speaking of libraries ...

I may be old school, but I strongly encourage you to read as many leadership books as you can, not just this one. As our thirty-third President Harry Truman famously said: "Not all readers are leaders, but all leaders are readers."[42]

Not sure what to read? Regularly check to see what's on *The New York Times* Business Best Sellers list; it's usually filled with leadership books. Also, publications such as *Entrepreneur* and *Inc.* regularly publish lists and reviews of recommended leadership books.

Don't enjoy reading or don't have the time to read? Consider listening to audiobooks during your commute or workouts. You also can visit YouTube or other video-streaming sites and watch videos on leadership, many of which feature famous leaders discussing concepts from their published works. And it seems just about everyone (except for yours truly) has a podcast these days. That means you can listen to or stream thousands of leadership and management episodes.

A second critical step in nurturing your leadership development is ***working with a trusted coach and/or mentor***. This person can be inside or outside your organization. The coaching and mentoring sessions can be formal or informal. And you can try it for a fixed amount of time or make it an ongoing process. The only thing that matters is that you find the right fit. Because this is such an important topic, I'll explore it more deeply in Lesson 10.

I also recommend ***joining professional organizations that focus on leadership*** and take advantage of their membership benefits, including attending their conferences. I belong to the Association of Talent Development, the International Leadership Association, The Greenleaf Center for Servant-Leadership, and the Society for Organizational Learning—all of which provide great leadership resources as part of my membership fees.[43]

Finally, research shows that ***engaging in reflection activities*** will shorten your developmental learning curve. These could include:

- Keeping a professional/leadership-development journal,
- Practicing formal mindfulness activities, or
- Blocking out informal reflection or quiet time on your calendar.

Ultimately, the method doesn't matter. The reflection does.

Follow these four general steps to your leadership development, and you'll be well on your way to discovering your individual magic formula.

LESSON 10:

Even Great Marathoners and Leaders Still Need Coaches or Mentors.

DEENA KASTOR IS ARGUABLY THE GREATEST US female marathoner ever. She won a bronze medal at the 2004 Olympics and has run the fourth fastest American women's marathon in history, winning the 2006 London Marathon in 2:19:36 (a 5:19 pace).[44]

But none of those things would have happened without a life-changing phone call with a running coach. After finishing a successful, but injury-plagued, running career at the University of Arkansas in 1996, Kastor was burned out, had quit running completely, and was considering opening a bakery in Fayetteville.

Fortunately, one of her former coaches asked her to call legendary running coach Joe Vigil before quitting the sport. After that first phone call with Coach Vigil, she threw on her running shoes and went for her first run in weeks. She came back from that run so reenergized that she packed up and moved to Alamosa, Colorado, to work full time with Vigil.

The rest, as they say, is history.

World-class athletes like Deena Kastor are not the only professionals who can benefit from coaching. Leaders at all levels of an organization should consider working with a qualified leadership coach, even if they're already highly successful leaders. After all, the world's greatest athletes continue to work with coaches until they retire from their sport, realizing they can always get better with the right guidance.

But if you're not ready to hire your own leadership coach, at least find a trusted mentor. Not sure what the difference is between the two? Let me clarify that for you.

Coaching Versus Mentoring

People often view coaching and mentoring as the same thing, and they do share a few common characteristics.[45] For example, both coaches and mentors will:

- Draw on their relevant training, formal education, and experience to help you;
- Clarify their roles and specific approaches prior to working with you;
- Build a relationship with you based on trust, respect, and compatibility; and
- Help you achieve both individual and organizational goals.

But like leadership and management, coaching and mentoring are not identical. Each serves a different purpose in your development, so it's more than an exercise in semantics to understand the differences between them. (See **Figure 8: Coaching Versus Mentoring** on the next page.)

Figure 8: Coaching Versus Mentoring

COACHING	MENTORING
Is a short-term, formal, and structured professional engagement	Is a long-term, informal, and flexible professional/personal relationship
Is almost always a compensated arrangement	Is almost always a voluntary connection
Focuses on specific skill sets and behavioral development	Focuses on general skill sets and career development
Involves regularly scheduled meetings with a structure or agenda	Involves flexible meetings in terms of recurrence, length, and focus
Uses formal assessments, goals, and measurements of progress	Uses informal dialogues about personal and professional experience
Requires expertise in specific skill sets	Requires expertise in a specific industry, role, and/or job level
Is coach driven	Is mentee driven
Usually terminates when agreed-upon results are achieved	Usually remains open-ended, sometimes lasting for years

Choosing the Right Coach

When looking for the right leadership coach, consider the following:

1. *Compatibility:* You and your coach don't have to be bosom buddies. In fact, you shouldn't be; otherwise, it may be difficult for each of you to deliver or receive corrective feedback. However, you and your coach DO need to have chemistry, so make sure you feel comfortable interacting with one another. Take it from someone who has coached hundreds of professionals: If the coach/coachee dynamic isn't a good fit, you're both wasting time, energy, and resources.

2. *Expertise:* Leadership and executive coaching is an unregulated industry, which means anyone can call themselves a coach, create a website, and start marketing their services. So you should check the qualifications of anyone you're considering working with. This includes their education, training, and experience. And while coaching may be unregulated, there are professional certifications coaches can achieve. These include the Associate Certified Coach (ACC), Professional Certified Coach (PCC), and Master Certified Coach (MCC) from the International Coach Federation (ICF)—one of the most respected coaching organizations in the world.[46] Keep in mind, however, that a coaching accreditation does not guarantee competency. I've heard horror stories about coaches who were accredited but incompetent. Therefore ...

3. *Recommendations or Client Referrals:* Most of my coaching engagements are referrals from satisfied clients. But when I do get an inquiry from one of my marketing efforts, I'm happy to put them in touch with current or former clients who have agreed to serve as references. This is common practice in the industry, so it should raise a red flag if a prospective coach refuses a request for references.

4. *Philosophy, Process, and Methodology:* All reputable coaches should be able to clearly and succinctly share their approach to coaching

with you. For example, I use a four-step process in all my coaching engagements:[47]

- **An initial conversation to determine our compatibility and to discuss your reasons for wanting one-on-one coaching;**
- **A review of recent 360 data or feedback you may have, or the completion of an assessment (or assessments) to provide benchmark data;**
- **A coaching plan based on the results of the 360 data, feedback, or assessment(s); and**
- **A package of coaching sessions using the most appropriate technique(s) for the situation.**

I also clarify the frequency, length, and confidentiality guidelines of our potential coaching sessions with the prospective client right up front.

Choosing the Right Mentor

As a first step, see if your organization has a formal mentoring program. If they do, sign up for it. If they don't, reach out to individuals in your professional network and find an informal mentor. (Even if you get assigned a formal mentor through your organization, I still recommend you work with an informal mentor to draw on multiple perspectives and approaches.)

In terms of specifics, consider the following:

1. *Compatibility:* Because mentoring is a long-term, informal relationship, having a personal connection with your mentor is even more important than having a personal connection with your coach. So, make sure you feel comfortable with each other. Remember, mentoring is all about an informal relationship that may last for years, so chemistry and comfort with each other are critical. It helps if you share similar attitudes, beliefs, and values. For example, if you're looking for help in developing your servant-leadership skills,

having a mentor with a power-based view of leadership would be a horrible fit.

2. *Expertise:* As I mentioned in **Figure 8**, the best mentors typically have experience in your industry. But even if they don't, they should at least have lots of experience in the same type of role or job level. Otherwise, their advice may not be as valuable as you would like. Having said that, I also encourage you to consider a mentor with experience in the role or job level you aspire to, not just the role or job level you're currently filling.

3. *Commitment and Availability:* Because mentoring is a long-term relationship, good mentors are both committed to and available for their mentees. Therefore, approach individuals who will not be difficult to connect with. More than one person has told me they were excited to work with a well-known or well-respected mentor, only to discover they could never get any of their time.

The best advice I can give you in terms of finding the right coach or mentor is to follow Deena Kastor's example and look for the individual(s) who best fits your personality, development needs, and career goals. Because if you find that perfect fit, magic can happen.

LESSON 11:

How You Carry Yourself Matters.

BECAUSE INDIVIDUALS HAVE BEEN RUNNING since they were small children, many tend to think their running form is naturally efficient. But that rarely is the case. Most runners have one or more serious flaws in their stride, feet strike, arm swing, or head position.

These flaws in running form waste a tremendous amount of energy and effort, which significantly affects performance. And if the flaws are bad enough, they can even lead to serious injury. So how runners carry themselves matters tremendously.

That's true for leaders as well.

How you carry yourself greatly determines how others view you as a leader. Specifically, it will go a long way in determining how much personal power people grant you, which is a critical component of your leadership success.

Power: The Currency of Leadership

In 1959, social psychologists John R. P. French and Betram Raven published the results of a study on social influence and power. In this groundbreaking work, the two men defined *social influence* as "the ability of an individual to change others' beliefs, attitudes, or behaviors." And they defined *power* as "the potential for that influence."[48]

Nearly every definition and discussion of power since French and Raven has been influenced by their work.[49] For example, I adhere to the now widespread definition of *power* as "the currency of leadership." But I have a slightly different take on it.

In the old leader-first and organization-as-machine mindsets, this currency was analogous to financial currency. Leaders spent, exchanged, and saved power. And the more power currency a leader had accumulated, the more likely they were to effectively influence the beliefs, attitudes, or behaviors of others.

What's more, power was viewed as "power over" others and a zero-sum game driven by organizational culture, hierarchy, and one's position in that hierarchy. For one leader to gain some power, another one had to lose some power. Consequently, in the decades following French and Raven's findings, generations of leaders focused on winning the zero-sum power game by accumulating as much position power currency as possible.

Personal Power

In the modern world of servant-leadership and organizations as living systems, power is still viewed as currency. However, it's now like electrical currency—a force that connects and energizes people.

Because this type of currency is generated by the leader, not granted by the organization, it is *not* a zero-sum game. Individuals can increase their personal power without having to drain that power currency from another source. Yes, power accorded by one's position still matters. But what ultimately determines how influential a leader becomes is the energy generated by their personal power, which is granted by the people with whom a leader interacts. In other words, how leaders carry themselves matters.

To help leaders increase this modern type of power currency, I developed the P.O.W.E.R.™ model, which is an acronym for the following five types of personal power:

P   *Presence:* The perception that you are articulate, self-assured, polished, attractive, and deserving of trust and respect

O   *Outcomes:* The perception that you consistently perform at a high level and regularly achieve superior results

W   *Willingness:* The perception that you are a hard worker, driven by a strong desire to succeed, and that you are willing to step out of your personal comfort zone by tackling new or challenging tasks to help your team or the organization

E   *Expertise:* The perception that you possess subject-matter knowledge, experience, and skill sets that others do not

R   *Relationships:* The perception that you have strong interpersonal skills that build connections and networks with customers, managers, peers, and direct reports

I could easily fill the rest of this book with a detailed discussion of personal power. But, for now, I'll simply wrap up this lesson with a quick review of its importance, as well as a few examples of how you can intentionally build or unintentionally destroy your personal power.

The Importance of Personal Power

Since French and Raven's 1959 study, leadership researchers have explored the importance of both position and personal power on a leader's success. And the findings are clear: personal power is much more ... well, powerful, than is position power. As is clearly illustrated in **Figure 9: Possible**

Responses to Personal P.O.W.E.R. below, you are much more likely to get commitment (rather than mere compliance) from people when you have personal power with them. And you will rarely encounter outright resistance from people with whom you have personal power.

Figure 9: Possible Responses to Personal P.O.W.E.R.

TYPE OF P.O.W.E.R.	Commitment	Compliance	Resistance
Presence			
Outcomes			
Willingness			
Expertise			
Relationships			

= Most Likely Response | = Possible Respone
= Least Likely Response

People will respond to your use of power in one of the following three ways:

1. *Commitment:* People enthusiastically respond positively to your influence attempts because they **WANT** to.
2. *Compliance:* People reluctantly respond positively to your influence attempts because they **HAVE** to.
3. *Resistance:* People deliberately respond negatively to your influence attempts because they neither **WANT** to nor believe they **HAVE** to.

So, like the marathoner who works on eliminating any serious flaws in their stride, feet strike, arm swing, or head position, you should spend a great deal of time focusing on how you carry yourself as a leader. And building deep reserves of personal power currency is the best place to start. (See **Figure 10: Examples of Building or Destroying Your P.O.W.E.R.** below.)

Figure 10: Examples of Building or Destroying Your P.O.W.E.R.

TYPE OF P.O.W.E.R.	EXAMPLE OF BUILDING	EXAMPLE OF DESTROYING
Presence	Taking a presentation skills course	Dressing inappropriately for your organization's culture
Outcomes	Underpromising and overdelivering	Missing deadlines or delivering poor quality work
Willingness	Displaying enthusiasm for challenges	Avoiding stretch opportunities
Expertise	Attending professional conferences	Being condescending to others
Relationships	Networking at organizational functions	Name-dropping

LESSON 12:

You're Going to Have Good Days and Bad Days. So Try Not to Get Too High or Too Low.

TRAINING FOR A MARATHON IS A SLOG. The shortest recommended training plans are sixteen weeks, but first-time marathoners are better served by twenty- or twenty-four-week programs.

Over those four-to-six months, runners are going to have great days when they feel like they're floating on air with the wind at their backs. But they're also going to have days when their legs are dead, and it feels like they're trudging through a sea of oatmeal.

That's why I encourage runners to stay emotionally grounded after both exhilarating and excruciating workouts. Each is going to happen over the course of a long training program. There's no sense spending too much emotional energy obsessing over what went so right or so wrong.

Your leadership days will be like that as well. There will be days when you can do no wrong. You will have the right answer to every question ... the brilliant solution to every problem ... the perfect one-liner that breaks the tension in the high-visibility, cross-functional meeting.

And then the pendulum will swing to the other extreme, and you'll wonder why you EVER thought you would be a good leader. Your staff is upset with you. Your peers are being totally unreasonable. And your boss? Let's not even go there!

Now, if these "terrible, horrible, no good, very bad" days become common (either when training for a marathon or leading in an organization), it may indeed be time to do some self-reflection about your approach. Or maybe you need to check in with your coach or mentor and get an objective take on what you could do differently.

However, most of the time you're simply experiencing the natural, albeit frustrating, ebb and flow of trying to master a difficult skill. And as I pointed out in Lesson 6, if it were easy, anyone could do it. But then it wouldn't mean as much.

The key is to stay centered and maintain emotional balance. How do you do that? By developing and demonstrating emotional intelligence.

Emotional Intelligence (or Emotional Quotient-EQ)

I base most of my one-on-one coaching engagements on improving my client's EQ, knowing that improved leadership skills will follow. I even joke that this coaching approach is straight from the classic film *Field of Dreams*: "If you build it (EQ) they (leadership skills) will come."

So, what exactly is EQ?

Basically, it is a combination of two general competencies (Personal and Social) and two desired outcomes (Awareness and Management) that create four critical skills for success: Self-Awareness, Self-Management, Social Awareness, and Relationship Management. (See **Figure 11** on the next page.)[50]

Don't be fooled by this simple definition. EQ is a powerful concept. In fact, as Travis Bradberry and Jean Graves report in their book, *Emotional Intelligence 2.0*, decades of research have concluded EQ is *the single greatest predictor of overall performance and leadership success in all types of jobs and professions.* Specifically:

- EQ directly accounts for 58% of a person's overall performance, regardless of job level or industry.
- 90% of high performers are also high in EQ, while just 20% of low performers are high in EQ.
- On average, people with high EQ earn $29,000 per year more than individuals with low EQ, and every point increase in EQ correlates to an average increase in salary of $1,300 a year.[51]

To increase your EQ skills, I recommend attending a training session facilitated by a certified instructor and/or start working with a certified coach. The two top EQ programs are Multi Health Systems' MHS EQi 2.0 and TalentSmart's Emotional Intelligence 2.0.[52] I'm certified in the MHS program, but you can't go wrong with either one of them.

Figure 11: Emotional Intelligence

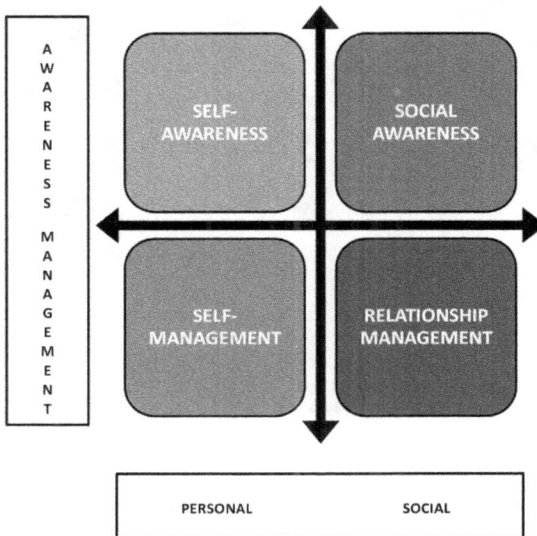

In the meantime, I'll wrap up this lesson with a few tips, techniques, and reminders on emotional self-awareness and expression, shown in **Figure**

12 below. I share these with all of my coachees because they're simple, yet powerful, concepts anyone can immediately apply.

Figure 12: Effective Emotional Self-Awareness and Expression

The following tips, techniques, and reminders will help you process and express your emotions more effectively.

1. Look for patterns in your emotional states. Are there certain "triggers" that you consistently respond to with negative emotions? Research shows that emotionally intelligent people actually anticipate these emotional triggers, which helps them better respond to them.

2. Clearly and accurately identify what specific emotion (anger, frustration, disappointment …) you're feeling before you try to express it to others.

3. Make sure you're in an appropriate emotional state to communicate your emotions (e.g., not too angry to clearly articulate that anger). As author Ambrose Bierce once wisely noted: "Speak when you are angry and you will make the best speech you will ever regret."

4. Choose an appropriate time and place to discuss your emotions.

5. Pay attention to your self-talk. Often, the way we talk to ourselves determines how strongly we feel our emotions. In general, negative self-talk leads to negative emotions, and that negativity will affect how we communicate those emotions.

6. As part of #5, avoid guessing people's intentions. Accusing others of bad intentions increases both your negative self-talk and their defensiveness. Having said that …

7. Don't be afraid to point out "intent versus impact" to others. The impact of their words and actions may not have been what they intended, but they need to own both.

8. Take ownership when others point out the impact of your words and actions, regardless of what your intent was.

9. Engage in a cost–benefit analysis of expressing your emotions to assess whether you want to express them to others.

10. "Do unto others as you would have them do unto you." Engage in empathy before expressing your emotions by imagining what it would feel like to hear the words you're about to use. On the other hand …

11. Don't get SO concerned about how others will respond to you expressing your emotions that you are too afraid to do so.

12. Begin with "I" statements when expressing your emotions. These force you to take responsibility for your emotions, and also prevent you from starting with "you" statements, which typically raise defensiveness in others: *"I'm angry …"* versus *"You made me angry …"*

13. After your "I" statement, identify the triggering or activating event: *"I'm angry that you missed the Acme contract deadline after consistently telling me everything was on track …"*

14. Make the connection between your emotional reaction and the triggering or activating event clear by providing some reason or rationale to the other individual(s) using a "because" statement: *"I'm angry that you missed the Acme contract deadline after consistently telling me everything was on track, because we're going to lose it. And that will have a huge impact on our Q3 revenue."*

15. Ensure your words and nonverbal behaviors match the emotion; otherwise, you may send contradictory/mixed messages (e.g., saying that "everything is fine" while standing there with your arms crossed and a scowl on your face).

16. Be precise in your word choice. Nothing is gained by speaking about your emotions in generalities.

17. Set a good example. If you respond in a sensitive/respectful way toward others when they express their emotions, they are more likely to respond in a sensitive/respectful way when you express yours.

18. **ALWAYS REMEMBER: NO ONE "MAKES YOU FEEL" AN EMOTION. WE CHOOSE OUR EMOTIONAL RESPONSES TO THE BEHAVIORS OF OTHERS.**

LESSON 13:

Practice "Association" (Doing) and "Disassociation" (Being).

I'VE COMPLETED THOUSANDS OF TRAINING RUNS over my three decades of running. Most of these sessions were quickly forgotten once I recorded them in my workout log. But every once in a while, a training run left an indelible impression on me, such as the run I mentioned in the *Introduction*, during which the seed for this book was planted.

Another memorable training run happened in July 2008. To escape the summer heat in Denver, I hit the trails of Rocky Mountain National Park near Estes Park, Colorado, for some cooler, high-altitude training.

At one point late in the run, I realized I had gone about three miles in what I can best describe as a trance. I didn't remember any of the beautiful scenery I had passed. I didn't recall thinking about anything. And I didn't notice my breathing, pace, or form, even though I had just covered a significant amount of difficult terrain.

That evening as I recorded the run in my workout log, I tried to process what I had experienced on the trail. I concluded I had experienced what professional athletes and sports psychologists call "the zone," which is a state wherein peak performance comes naturally.

This experience led me to learn all I could about "the zone" (or "flow," as it's often referred to) in the hopes I could foster these moments of peak performance during my workouts and races. I developed and began practicing two different training techniques based on what I learned: "association" (doing) and "disassociation" (being).[53] These techniques became a foundation for the training plans I developed for the athletes I coached. And like all the topics in this book, they were easy to apply in my leadership coaching as well.

Association (Doing)

In a running context, association involves consciously focusing on your pace, stride, breathing, arm swing, head position, and thirst or hunger levels, so you can adjust as necessary. Failure to engage in association during a workout or race can result in wasted energy, incorrect pacing, decreased performance, and even injury.

When my runners struggle to associate, I recommend they imagine they're wearing a microphone and are being filmed for a running video. Because they'll need to demonstrate ideal form, breathing, pacing, etc. for the video, this forces them to focus their attention instead of letting it wander.

I take a similar approach with the leaders I coach.

The first step in teaching association techniques to leaders is identifying a key development area that they need to work on. Next, we break down that development area into specific behavioral skills they can engage in to improve in that area. The leaders then consciously choose moments during their daily routines when they practice these skills, all the while imagining they are being filmed for a leadership training video. This forces the leaders to both practice the targeted skills and monitor how they feel while engaged in that practice.

You may already be familiar with the concept of association but know it by a different name: mindfulness. One of the rising trends in leadership and management training (especially during the COVID-19 pandemic), mindfulness is both a state of being and a set of specific skills designed to help individuals stay focused on the present.

If you're interested in learning more about mindfulness, I've provided some great resources in the *References* section that concludes this book.[54] For now, just remember that association is a critical skill for runners at all distances. But because the marathon is so long, marathoners must also learn how to disassociate. And as we learned in Lesson 1, leadership is a marathon, so leaders must learn how to disassociate as well.

Disassociation (Being)

Disassociation is simply going on sensory autopilot. It's letting go of all conscious thoughts and concerns, including everything I mentioned previously. When done correctly, this allows runners to experience "the zone" or "flow" by simply being, not doing.

Most beginning marathoners learn disassociation fairly quickly. Many leaders, however, struggle mightily with it. I think it's a control issue for most people. Letting go and simply being means the leader is not trying to control everything and everyone around them, including themselves. And that's scary for a lot of individuals.

But it's a skill all leaders must learn if they're going to become marathon leaders. You simply cannot be in association mode all the time. For one thing, it's exhausting. Show me a leader who can't disassociate, and I'll show you one destined for burnout. It's also the surest way to become a micromanager. And no one wants that to happen, especially your direct reports.

So, how do you learn to disassociate if you're not good at it?

I mentioned during the association section that I have my runners and leaders imagine they are being filmed for a training video. That mindset forces them to be hyperaware of their actions, which is the very definition of association.

To learn disassociation, I teach my runners and leaders to do the exact opposite. Instead of imagining themselves as the center of attention, I encourage them to imagine they are audience members observing a play or movie. This technique forces them to focus on things outside of themselves, including the tasks they need to complete and the people they interact with.

Part of that focusing outside of yourself is allowing your five physical senses, not your mind, to take over. This is easier said than done, because every second you're alive, a soundtrack is playing in your brain. But shutting down that soundtrack so you can use your physical senses of seeing, hearing, feeling, smelling, and tasting is critical for disassociating.

To practice this, choose moments during your day to focus on what your senses are feeding you, *without* trying to analyze those sensory inputs. (That would be association.) Instead, just experience them. When a thought or sensory interpretation does enter your brain, such as, "I wish this meeting would end soon because I have so much to do" or "I wonder if I should just do this myself," push it out of your mind by refocusing on the sensory signals you're picking up.

One thing that may help you disassociate is replacing your thoughts with a mantra, a word or phrase that you repeat over and over again to block out conscious thoughts. I use the phrase "See and Be" when I want to disassociate. One of my leaders came up with "Thee Not Me" to help him shut down his thoughts and simply be. Yet another executive visualizes a certain shade of pink, allowing the color to fill her mind instead of words. With practice, you'll find that you can shut down your internal soundtrack and begin just experiencing, not thinking.

Again, I realize this is a high-level introduction to what is a complex practice. That's why I've also included some great resources on the zone/flow in the *References* section. I'll also introduce you to other disassociation techniques in two future lessons. These include delegating to others (Lesson 18) and overcoming your fears (Lesson 24).

However, none of these techniques will teach you disassociation if you're unwilling to give up control. Therefore, the first step I recommend is heeding the advice of Elsa in Disney's *Frozen* and just "let it go."

LESSON 14:
Keep It Simple.

A FEW YEARS AGO, MY WIFE AND I were having dinner in Boulder with my late friend Ed Craighead the night before he ran the BOLDERBoulder 10K. Ed, who hailed from Amarillo, Texas, was a BOLDERBoulder age-group legend well into his seventies. Year after year, he won, or (occasionally) finished second, in his age group at one of the largest and most competitive races in the country. So, he knew a thing or two about running.

Naturally, we were talking running over dinner. Well, I was talking running. Ed was mostly listening as I discussed the training plan I had put together for Kathy's upcoming first marathon. While I reviewed the various workouts I had designed for Kathy, Ed sat there quietly eating. He nodded politely as I waxed on about VO2 max, the importance of training periodization, and the challenge of maintaining heart rate training zones.

When I finally finished, he looked at me, paused, and said in his quiet Texas drawl: "Gee, David, you make it all sound so complicated. I just run."

Talk about the proverbial 2 X 4 of enlightenment smacking me across the forehead! Ed was right. I was way overcomplicating something that should have been relatively simple.

After that dinner with Ed, I simplified the training plans I developed for Kathy and the other runners I was coaching. More importantly, I started noticing how many of the leaders I was working with were doing the exact same thing in their organizations. Instead of keeping things simple, they were overengineering processes, procedures, and projects to the detriment of all. Because the simpler the system, the better it usually works.

Leadership and Simplicity

I'm certainly not the only person preaching the gospel of simplicity to modern leaders. For example, management guru Tom Peters once observed that "almost all quality improvement comes via simplification of design, manufacturing, layout, processes, and procedures."[55] And Steve Jobs viewed simplicity as a foundation to both individual leadership and organizational success:

"That's been one of my mantras—focus and simplicity. Simple can be harder than complex: You have to work hard to get your thinking clean to make it simple. But it's worth it in the end because once you get there, you can move mountains."[56]

Research supports these legends' views.

A landmark study conducted by Steve Strelsin (himself a CEO) in partnership with the Harvard Business School looked at the behaviors of CEOs in relation to their records of achievement.[57] The CEOs of successful, often industry-leading companies consistently listed simplifying the lives of those who worked below them as their number one priority. Specifically, these CEOs:

- Simplified their strategies so their people and the entire organization focused only on what really mattered;
- Simplified their organizational structure, processes, and procedures so their people could execute their strategies more effectively; and
- Simplified their communication so that everyone was clear about the above two items.

These findings led Lisa Bodell, author of *Why Simple Wins*, to conclude that successful CEOs are effective because they view themselves first and foremost as Chief Simplicity Officers.

So, how do *you* keep it simple? Bodell recommends the following:

1. Create a clear vision.
2. Embed simplicity into your strategy.
3. Streamline management layers.
4. Simplify decision-making.
5. Establish clear metrics.
6. Build a simplification team.[58]

Although some of the items on Bodell's list are directed toward the C-suite, most of them can be applied by all leaders. Because keeping it simple for your people is important for leaders at any level. In fact, authors Tom Schmitt and Arnold Perl claim in their book *Simple Solutions: Harness the Power of Passion and Simplicity to Get Results* that simplicity is the foundation of ALL leadership.[59] And I agree.

So, I now preach the KISS gospel to every leader and organization I work with: Keep It Simple, Stupid. For the most part, people take my advice. And you should too. Whenever you face a choice between the simple and the complex, always go for the simple. It's what Ed would have done.

LESSON 15:
Both Marathoners and Leaders Need to Be Good Listeners.

DURING A RUNNING-COACH CERTIFICATION COURSE years ago, one of the facilitators said something that resonated deeply with me: "Listen to your body's whispers, so it doesn't have to scream." What she meant was that runners need to listen to what their bodies are subtly telling them in terms of energy levels and minor aches and pains *before* they turn into exhaustion or injuries from overtraining.

Not only have I passed on that wisdom to the athletes I've coached over the years, I've applied it to my own training, especially now that I'm in my sixties. Because the reality is that some days my body tells me it can't complete the hard workout I have scheduled. So instead of risking injury, I either switch out my scheduled workout, reduce its intensity, or skip it altogether and take a day off. And while listening to my body's whispers may be temporarily frustrating, it's a lot better than waiting until it screams at me in the form of an injury.

Like marathoners, leaders must be great listeners. For as we learned in Lesson .2, effective listening is a foundational skill of servant-leadership.

But despite the importance of listening, most leaders (heck, most humans) are horrible at it. In fact, of all the skills I teach or coach, active listening is by far the one that most leaders believe they're better at than they actually are. So I spend a lot of time teaching leaders how to better practice this critical leadership skill, knowledge I'm happy to now pass on to you.[60]

To become a better listener, practice the following four steps of active listening:

Step 1: Pay Attention

One of the main reasons we're such horrible listeners is that we don't give our full attention to what others are trying to communicate. So the first step in effective active listening is to practice the following attentive behaviors:

- Do not multitask, so you can give the speaker your full attention. (Yes, that means putting down your phone and looking away from your computer screen.)
- Face the other person directly, keeping an open posture.
- Maintain eye contact.
- Limit fidgeting.
- Remain silent to allow the other person to share their facts and feelings without interruption.
- Turn off your internal soundtrack or counter-arguer.

Step 2: Listen for Real Meaning

Another reason we struggle to listen effectively is that we confuse it with simply hearing and processing the words used by the individuals with whom we're communicating. However, listening for *real* meaning requires paying close attention to all three of the following:

- The other person's *words*.
- The other person's *nonverbal behaviors*.
- The other person's *emotional state*.

Specifically, I encourage you to look for any inconsistencies in these three channels, recognizing that when a person is experiencing discomfort, frustration, or anger, it is common to get mixed messages from them. Also, keep in mind that it may take some time before the real meaning or message surfaces. So, try to be patient. And always remember this important equation:

Words + Nonverbal Behaviors + Emotions = Real Meaning

Step 3: Communicate Your Understanding of What You Heard

As you listen for the real meaning, it is important to verify your perceptions by communicating your understanding of what you *think* you heard the other person say. Initially, you should be careful not to interpret what the other person said; instead, focus simply on paraphrasing back the words they shared with you. By using the following active listening formula, you will be less likely to interpret too early in the conversation.

- **"You feel"** or **"You are feeling"** (describe the feeling)
- **"About"** (describe the experiences/behaviors that underlie the feeling).
- You can paraphrase the feeling portion of the active listening formula with:
- A word ("So you feel confused about …")
- A phrase ("So what you're saying is that you feel all mixed up about …")
- A "like" phrase ("So what I'm hearing is that you feel like the world is coming to an end because …")

Remember: Effective active listeners do not attempt to provide "solutions" to the other party's concern or problem until they thoroughly and effectively understand the other party's concern or problem.

One final note about paraphrasing …

I believe active listening has gotten a bad rap because when we first started teaching the skills, we did so in a rote, formulaic fashion, especially this third step. The line, "So what I hear you saying is …" became so forced and unnatural that people stopped checking for understanding at all. That's why I encourage you to use words and phrases that sound natural coming out of your mouth. Otherwise, the individuals you're communicating with may perceive you as not really engaged in or sincere about your active listening.

Step 4: Probe Deeper (If Necessary)

This fourth step is only necessary if you detect an inconsistency between a person's words, nonverbal behaviors, and feelings. If you do, carefully probe deeper (a technique often referred to as "tagging"). The following are a few suggestions for probing deeper into a topic:

- "I hear you saying everything is okay, but I also hear anxiety in your voice. Is there something you're worried about?"
- "You tell me you're comfortable with this decision, but you have your arms crossed and look angry. Are you sure you're okay with this?"
- "You say that everything is fine, but you still sound frustrated to me. Is there something wrong?"
- "You told me you're excited about this, but I don't hear that in your voice. Are you hesitant about something?"

Learning and effectively applying these four critical active listening skills will allow you to hear other people's whispers so they don't have to scream at you. And who doesn't want to avoid that?

PART THREE:
Racing Principles

FOR MARATHONERS, ONE OF THE MOST FRUSTRATING aspects of the COVID-19 pandemic was the cancellation of most races after mid to late March 2020 and much of 2021. Yes, race directors tried to fill the void with virtual races. But let's face it. Virtual races are just training runs you pay for to get a medal and other race swag. For most of us, this dearth of actual races meant it was hard to stay focused on our training. There simply wasn't a tangible payoff for all that hard work.

It's not all that different for leaders.

The reason you train hard to become a great leader is to see that effort pay off in your day-to-day leadership moments. Without those rewarding moments, the journey to leadership greatness loses its purpose, and your motivation to complete it can lag. The nine lessons in Part Three focus on your leadership "races"—those real-world opportunities to apply all your training and hard work to successfully lead others. For example, in Lesson 16 I'll discuss how leadership opportunities are as unique as marathon courses, which means you need to approach each one differently. Lessons 17 and 18 reinforce this critical skill of leadership agility at both the organizational and individual levels. In Lessons 19 and 20, I'll ask you to think outside of yourself and focus on others during your leadership journey, just as marathoners need to consider competitors and race volunteers during their races.

Finally, Lessons 21, 22, 23, and 24 are all about you and the deeply personal aspects of completing a marathon or being a great leader. That includes facing your fears of failure and dealing with "the wall" (the obstacles that make you want to quit).

LESSON 16:

Leadership Opportunities Are Like Marathon Courses. Each One Is Unique and Should Be Approached Differently.

ALTHOUGH THE DISTANCE OF EVERY certified marathon course is the same 26 miles, 385 yards, no two courses are identical in terms of terrain, typical weather conditions, and number of runners.

For example:

- Some courses are well known for their punishing hills (Athens, Greece, Boston, and Crater Lake, OR).
- Others offer fast downhill or flat courses that help runners achieve personal bests (Chicago, Houston, and the Revel series).
- Still others have unpredictable or predictably brutal weather conditions (Laramie, WY, with its legendary wind; Kona, HI, with its merciless heat and humidity; and Antarctica with its bitter cold and deadly storms).

- Large races (New York, Los Angeles, and London) require runners to take a very different approach than they would at smaller races.

Likewise, different leadership situations provide unique challenges, which means any leader employing a "one-size-fits-all" approach is destined to fail. So, you must develop leadership agility. This trait is so important to your success, I'll examine it in depth over the next three lessons, beginning with three key organizational variables that will affect your approach to leadership: size, culture, and level of responsibility.

Three Organizational Variables

The first key variable is the size of the organization in which a leader works.[61] Leadership in a 25-person Silicon Valley start-up looks considerably different from leadership in an established 100,000-employee multinational corporation. You should understand what you're getting yourself into before accepting a leadership opportunity in either.

For example, being a leader in a small organization (especially a start-up) means you're going to wear many different hats on a daily basis. That may include the expectation you'll be filling two full-time roles: being a manager AND an individual contributor. So you should expect some long days ... and nights.

The good news is that you'll never be bored leading in a small company. So, if you're the type of person who thrives on variety and even chaos, leading in that environment will be a good fit.

Conversely, leading in a large organization will probably allow you to wear fewer hats in your role. Large organizations also typically provide a bit more structure and stability than do small organizations and start-ups. However, leading in a large organization will also require you to have a lot more patience, because you'll have to navigate the labyrinths of hierarchy and bureaucracy that often pervade these types of organizations.

A second organizational variable is culture, which includes its values, explicit rules, and implicit norms. While a detailed discussion of culture is beyond the scope of this lesson, it is important for you to understand the general leadership culture of your organization.

For example, certain companies require their leaders to be by-the-book, hands-on managers who are deeply involved (and some would say *over*-involved) in day-to-day operations. Leading in these types of organizations means spending a lot of time in the right side of "The Leadership/Management Continuum" I introduced back in Lesson 1.

Other organizations ask their leaders to be more transformational and less transactional (the left side of the Continuum). These flatter, more collaborative-based organizations encourage even critical decisions to be made at all levels. And that can be challenging for leaders used to making all of the important decisions. In my experience, individuals who struggle with being a servant-leader do not survive long in these types of organizations, because even if they don't use the formal terminology, the culture emphasizes the spirit of servant-leadership.

Finally, ***an individual's level in the organization*** matters as well, because it determines which combination of the following three broad types of skills you'll need to focus on:

- Technical skills (task oriented)
- People skills (relationship oriented)
- Conceptual skills (strategy oriented)[62]

When you're an individual contributor, you generally are evaluated based on how well you execute the technical skills associated with your specific role. Yes, you'll need some people skills, and conceptual skills will be important for career advancement. But ultimately, it's all about how well you demonstrate your technical skills while completing your day-to-day tasks.

As a frontline supervisor or manager, you'll need to focus more on people skills and less on technical skills, while also developing your conceptual skills (again, especially if you hope to be promoted higher in the organization). Rising to the ranks of director, vice president, and certainly C-suite executive will require strong conceptual/strategic skills, some people skills, and just enough technical skills to understand what individuals at other levels of the organization face daily.

These three macro-level organizational variables *(size, culture,* and *level of responsibility)* will significantly influence your overall approach to leadership. But they are not the only variables that will require you to demonstrate leadership agility. Like great marathoners who modify their race strategies to the current internal and external conditions they face, you'll need to develop broad strategic agility skills. And you'll also have to daily (if not hourly!) adjust your specific leadership behaviors based on micro-level variables such as the individuals involved, the potential risks and consequences of their actions, and the politics inherent in the situation—agility topics I'll explore further in the next two lessons.

LESSON 17:

Always Have a Plan. But Don't Hesitate to Deviate from That Plan If Conditions Warrant It.

EXPERIENCED MARATHONERS APPROACH RACES with specific goals in mind, along with concrete pacing plans to reach those goals. But sometimes they're forced to alter those plans based on conditions outside of their control: weather, injury, illness, unexpected competition, etc. And if they don't adjust, they often pay dearly for their stubbornness.

For example, I ran the 2004 Los Angeles Marathon on a day of record heat. Wisely, I slowed my pace and increased my fluid intake from the start. But many other runners didn't make any adjustments, and by the final 5K I felt as if I were in a death march. Runners literally were dropping around me from dehydration and other heat-related problems. And because I was staying in a hotel right by the finish line, I heard the sirens of ambulances transporting heat-stricken runners to local hospitals for hours after I finished.

Similarly, too many leaders stick to a vision, strategic plan, or specific goals and objectives when it's obvious to everyone else that conditions have made them obsolete. But like the above-mentioned marathoners, these leaders refuse to adjust and stubbornly plow on, leaving widespread swaths of destruction in their wake.

Why? Often, it's ego. They wrongly believe that altering their original plans will imply those plans were somehow flawed to begin with. But great leaders don't see it that way. They realize their visions, strategic plans, or goals and objectives *must* be altered as conditions change.

Look at what happened in 2020 and 2021 due to the COVID-19 pandemic. Executives—especially in the travel, hospitality, restaurant, and fitness industries—were forced to alter all (and I mean ALL) aspects of their businesses. Revenue projections for the year? Useless. Strategic initiatives? Canceled. Targeted KPIs or objectives and key results (OKRs)? Irrelevant. But it shouldn't take a once-a-century worldwide pandemic to get leaders to be agile. Remember, leading in a living system means you're always going to be dealing with constantly changing conditions. That's why strategic agility is such a critical skill for twenty-first-century leaders.

Strategic Agility

At the organizational level, strategic agility is the ability of organizations to anticipate, recognize, or even invent new opportunities for their products or services.[63] This means creating new markets/opportunities with new products/services that reach new customers/clients. It differs from operational agility, which is simply improving existing products/services for existing customers/clients. To illustrate this important difference, see the examples in **Figure 13: Operational Agility Versus Strategic Agility** on the next page, which are from a 2018 article in *Forbes* magazine by Steven Denning.

Only organizations that demonstrate strategic agility will be able to survive, let alone thrive, as the pace of business continues to accelerate. And proactively recognizing opportunities and threats *before* they occur—along with responding and adjusting to those that come out of the blue, such as COVID-19—will require leaders to focus on multiple competencies. These competencies, which I'll cover in the remainder of this lesson, are not a "nice to have" for marathon leaders. They are a "must have."

Figure 13: Operational Agility Versus Strategic Agility

OPERATIONAL AGILITY	STRATEGIC AGILITY
Making a better candle	Inventing the light bulb
Breeding and training faster horses	Manufacturing the first automobile
Building better mobile phones	Developing the iPhone—an all-in-one phone, camera, and music player
Improving the quality and distributions of DVDs	Pioneering web-based streaming of movies

Strategic Agility Competencies

To help their organizations become more strategically agile, leaders must develop the following five individual strategic-agility competencies:

1. *Strategic Thinking:* Before leaders can become strategically agile, they first need to be capable of strategic thinking.[64] And that's easier said than done. According to the research, as well as my own experience coaching and training leaders, strategic-thinking skills are more difficult to teach and learn than are technical or people skills. But they are critical for your success. So, you'll need to develop specific skill sets, including systems thinking, data analysis and synthesis, critical thinking, decision-making, visioning, and foresight.

2. *Decisiveness:* In the world of strategic agility, the old expression "he who hesitates is lost" takes on increased importance. Strategic agility requires leaders to make decisions quickly, often without all the information they would like. And depending on your specific Meyers-Briggs, DiSC, or Enneagram profile (or any other personality or behavioral assessment), you may find this extremely uncomfortable. Those who suffer from bouts of "analysis paralysis" will especially need to remind themselves regularly that a fundamental part of being a strategically agile leader is recognizing that no decision will be perfect. But *any* decision often is better than no decision or a delayed decision.

3. *Embracing Change:* Today's leaders operate in a VUCA environment: Volatile, Uncertain, Complex, and Ambiguous. Successful leaders recognize they must not only be personally comfortable adapting to change, they also must know how to lead others through change. That means you'll need to develop world-class change-management skills.[65] And like decisiveness, those skills will be easier for some to build and apply than others.

4. *Risk Tolerance:* At some point during the development of your strategic-agility skills, you will need to work on the ability to quickly calculate risks and then decide what actions to take based on those risks. This will require you to first understand your natural comfort level with risk, which is usually identified by one of three labels: risk-averse, risk-neutral, or risk-seeking.[66] It will also require you to take the emotions out of risk-taking so you can see things as objectively as possible. This is not as easy as it sounds because risks naturally evoke a lot of emotions in us. But risks also provide incredible opportunity, so you must learn how to manage your fears around them.

5. *A Growth Mindset:* Although she is not the only researcher or writer on the subject, Carol S. Dweck popularized this concept in her bestseller *Mindset.*[67] In it, Dr. Dweck concludes that people can

be categorized as having either a fixed or growth mindset. Those with a fixed mindset believe their talents and abilities are relatively fixed from birth (more nature than nurture, using the terminology from Lesson 2). Because of this, they avoid anything outside of their comfort zones due to fear of failure or looking bad. This means people with fixed mindsets tend to plateau early and never fulfill their potential. On the other hand, those with a growth mindset believe in nurture over nature. They strive for constant improvement, thrive on challenges outside of their comfort zone, and accept critical feedback, mistakes, and even outright failures as natural steps along the journey to success. Obviously, strategic agility requires leaders with growth, not fixed, mindsets. The good news is that a growth mindset can be learned, so I encourage you to check out Dweck's suggestions/techniques for doing so.

A Final Analogy

For those of you still struggling to accept a leader's need for strategic agility, including the previously described five competencies, let me provide a final analogy that may help. If you were on a plane and saw a massive 36,000-foot thunderstorm up ahead, would you want the pilot to stubbornly fly through it and stick to the original flight plan? Or would you want them to adjust and fly around it? I'm guessing it's the latter.

That's all your people are asking you to do sometimes: steer the ship around the turbulence instead of through it. At a minimum, failure to do so will guarantee a bumpy ride for you and your followers. At its worst, failure to do so will result in crashing and burning.

LESSON 18:

Set the Pace for Others at Times. But Also Know When to Drop Back and Let Others Lead.

IF YOU WATCHED TELEVISION COVERAGE of the 2019 London Marathon, you saw eventual winner Eliud Kipchoge regularly pleading with other runners in the lead pack to take their turns being in front. But none of them would, including some of Kipchoge's own countrymen.

Their reluctance to do so was understandable. Kipchoge is one of the fastest marathoners ever, so his competitors wanted to "draft" behind him.

Drafting involves staying close behind another competitor to take advantage of their aerodynamic slipstream.[68] By doing so, the follower's effort is decreased, while the lead runner's workload is increased, because that leader is the first to encounter the atmospheric conditions (especially wind) that slow runners down.

Although drafting has a much bigger impact in the sport of cycling, it affects endurance running events as well. Research indicates that effective drafting during a marathon can improve a runner's performance by approximately 1%–2% in still conditions and significantly more on windy days. That can make a big difference in your marathon finish time, whether you're in the lead pack, main pack, or back of the pack working hard just to avoid the course cut-off time.

Like the lead runner in a pack, a leader is the first to encounter external challenges that can slow down the pace of a team, department, or the entire organization. They are forced to work harder than those following in their footsteps.

While that's a natural byproduct of the leadership process, effective leaders learn how to share this load with others by demonstrating agility in delegation and empowerment. And learning how you can do that more effectively is the focus of this lesson on leadership agility.

The R.A.N.™ Model of Performance Management

I developed the R.A.N.™ Model of Performance Management to help leaders diagnose and delegate more effectively. Based on the Contingency Theory of Leadership, R.A.N. is an acronym that stands for "Roles Addressing Needs" and is designed to help leaders accurately assess the current needs of their individual followers or teams and then adjust their leadership role to best address those needs.[69] In other words, it teaches leaders when to set the pace for others and when to drop back and let others take the lead.

Implementing the R.A.N. Model requires the leader to first identify where individuals or teams are on the two components of performance:

1. *Execution:* This is the objective, behavioral aspect of performance. Is the individual or team successfully performing *(the what)* in an acceptable way *(the how)*?
2. *Engagement:* This is the subjective, emotional aspect of performance. Does the individual or team want to perform at a high level *(motivation)* and believe they can perform at a high level *(confidence)*?

By accurately diagnosing the combination of these two variables, leaders can identify their individuals' or team's current stage of performance and their associated leadership needs. (See **Figure 14: The Five Stages of Performance** on page 102.) This helps leaders effectively determine who is ready to take the lead on a task, project, or initiative—and who is not. And that prompts the second step of the model: choosing the right performance-management role for the individual's or team's stage of performance.

Like the performance stages, the performance-management roles are determined by two different components:

1. *Direction:* This is the behavioral aspect of managing performance. Traditionally labeled "task orientation" or "task behavior" in management literature, it involves *doing* something to help individuals perform better. This might include walking them through a process step-by-step; setting specific goals, defining roles and responsibilities, and clarifying performance expectations for them; and correcting unacceptable behavior.

2. *Support:* This is the emotional aspect of managing performance. Traditionally labeled "relationship orientation" or "relationship behavior" in management literature, it involves *inspiring* your individual or team to perform better by praising and rewarding them; building their confidence and encouraging them; and co-sharing goal setting, role and responsibility defining, and performance setting with them.

Figure 14: The Five Stages of Performance

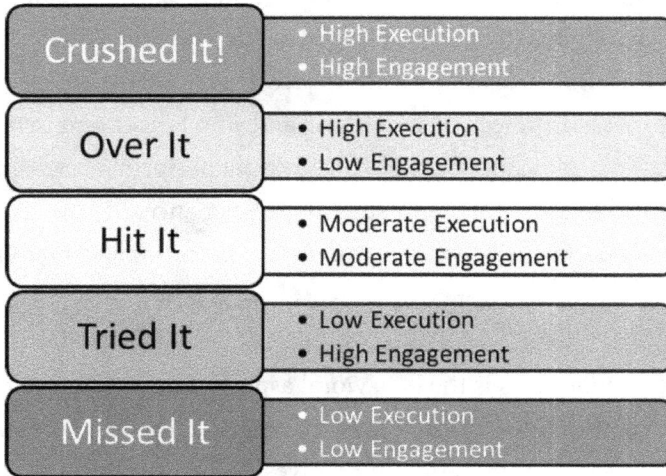

Crushed It!	• High Execution • High Engagement
Over It	• High Execution • Low Engagement
Hit It	• Moderate Execution • Moderate Engagement
Tried It	• Low Execution • High Engagement
Missed It	• Low Execution • Low Engagement

As was the case with the performance stages, the various combinations of these two components create five distinct performance-management roles. (See **Figure 15: The Five Performance-Management Roles** on the next page.) Research shows that matching the role most appropriate to the specific needs of each stage is the secret to effective delegation and high performance.

I realize the previous few pages are a basic, high-level summary of what is a complex, constantly fluctuating process. Obviously, I go into much more depth in my Marathon Leadership training sessions.

Figure 15: The Five Performance-Management Roles

Consultant	• Low Direction • Low Support
Cheerleader	• Low Direction • High Support
Counselor	• Moderate Direction • Moderate Support
Coach	• High Direction • High Support
Commander	• High Direction • Low Support

But even this brief introduction to the R.A.N. Model of Performance Management should help you accurately assess the current needs of your individual followers or teams and then adjust your leadership role to best address those needs. Because as Eliud Kipchoge can attest, it is critical for you to know when to set the pace for others and when to drop back and let others take the lead.

LESSON 19:

Competitors Are Wonderful Gifts. Embrace Them and Push Each Other to Greatness.

THE 2007 CHICAGO MARATHON is remembered for two things:

1. Unseasonable heat that eventually forced race officials to shut down the course, and
2. The greatest finish in marathon history.[70]

That hot October day, Patrick Ivuti, a twenty-nine-year-old Kenyan who had only run three prior marathons, overtook Morocco's Jaouad Gharib, thirty-five, a two-time world marathon champion, at the finish line. Ivuti's official time was 2 hours 11 minutes 11 seconds. Gharib's was 2:11:11.05 … a minuscule half-second difference over the course of 26.2 miles!

If you watch this amazing finish on YouTube, you can see how these two fierce competitors pushed each other toward the finish line.[71] They were the true definition of "compete," which comes from the Latin word *competere*, or "to seek together."[72] True competition isn't about destroying each other. It is about pushing each other to levels of effort and success that would have been impossible without that push.

In that spirit, I challenge my clients to reevaluate and realign how they view competitors. Instead of regarding them as enemies that must be destroyed at all costs (a negative mental model derived from warfare), I encourage them to embrace their competitors as worthy partners in a mutual quest for greatness (a positive mental model borrowed from racing).

Before you accuse me of being just another "touchy-feely" consultant who has no idea what it's like in the real world, let me make something clear. I'm NOT saying we shouldn't try to defeat our opponents, either on the racecourse or in the business world. I'm simply arguing that viewing competition as outright war, and our competitors as enemies, isn't the right mindset.

To illustrate this point, let me share two real-world examples with you. The first is how *not* to view your competition. The second shows how one of my clients reached a level of success that would have been impossible without the push from its competitors.

Don't Be THAT Guy

A few years ago, I was asked to speak about leadership at an event one of my Fortune 100 clients was holding for its regional employees. Before I took the stage for my presentation, one of the organization's executives spoke. In a speech that reminded me of a fire-and-brimstone sermon by an evangelical minister, the executive tore into their largest competitor (which I'll call "Acme").

During his lengthy tirade he literally screamed the following:

- "I don't dislike Acme. I HATE them!"
- "I hate them so much that when I'm walking down the street and come upon one of their locations, I cross to the other side, just so I don't have to go near them."

- "If they were the last organization left in our industry, I'd start a new career in a different industry. THAT'S how much I hate them!"
- "I don't want to beat Acme. I want to DESTROY them. This is war!"

Now, there's no denying he had whipped his audience into an enthusiastic frenzy by the time he was finished speaking. I, on the other hand, was absolutely aghast—so much so that it affected the first few minutes of my own presentation. All I kept asking myself was: *How can you function effectively with that much anger, hatred, and negative energy focused on your competitor?*

Interestingly, that executive exited the organization less than a year after I heard him speak. To be fair, I don't know if it was a voluntary or involuntary termination. But I can't imagine what it must have been like to work with him, let alone *for* him. (Heaven forbid!) So, I don't doubt for a moment that his scorched-earth personality left a lot of collateral damage in its wake and probably had something to do with his leaving.

I wish I could say this executive was an aberration. But my thirty-plus years as a leadership coach, trainer, and consultant (and twenty-plus years as a distance runner and triathlete) have shown me otherwise. The sad fact is that a lot of individuals truly believe the best way to win in business or in athletics is to develop a hatred for your competitor(s) and focus all your energies on obliterating them.

A Better Approach

One of my oldest and favorite clients was in a unique situation a few years ago, one you'd think most companies would dream of. This technology company basically was the first player in their industry and almost single-handedly created the market for their services, which were highly sought after by consumers. Sounds idyllic, doesn't it?

The problem with this utopian situation is that they were SO successful at building the market, they caught the attention of other technology companies in related industries, as well as a few start-ups. These competitors, especially the start-ups with their deep-pocketed venture-capitalist backers, recognized an incredible opportunity to enter that lucrative space. While these competitors ramped up their efforts to steal market share, my client consistently struggled to build upon its early successes.

Why?

Because they had spent so long without any competitors pushing them, they had become complacent and started underperforming. Trust me, the leadership team saw this happening and tried to implement organizational best practices around leading change, creating a sense of urgency, increasing employee engagement ... but nothing seemed to work.

Until one of their upstart competitors started luring away some of their clients.

Suddenly, the proverbial fire was lit. The entire organization rallied, and they began to perform at a high level—*without* leaders spewing hatred, obliteration, and war-filled diatribes.

On the contrary, the leadership team lit this fire by consciously embracing the new competition. They routinely shared competitor updates during their own all-hands meetings. In their internal communications, they openly expressed their concerns about *and* admiration for their competitors' technological advances. And they challenged their own employees to best those advances through their own creative thinking and technological innovations, an approach that invited healthy competition.

This approach worked. Granted, they're not entirely out of the woods. Like the marathoner who leads throughout the first 26 miles of the race only to be passed during the final .2 miles, they still are in danger of being caught and ultimately passed by competitors who outkick them.

However, they have significantly slowed the progress of their largest competitor in terms of market share. I have so much faith in their leadership team that I'm convinced they'll not only survive but thrive. One thing I *am* certain of is that without these new competitors pushing them, they would have continued along at a safe, comfortable pace until their organizational performance deteriorated to the point where it may not have been salvageable.

Remember: Whether it's Coke versus Pepsi, Apple versus Microsoft, Ford versus Chevy, McDonald's versus Burger King ... or a whole host of other great corporate rivalries, competition is healthy for organizations. It's what drives innovation and effort.

So, don't be like the executive I introduced you to a few pages ago. Instead, be like my technology client. Embrace your competitors as the precious gifts they are. And push each other to greatness.

LESSON 20:

Always Thank the People Who Help You Along the Way, Especially Your Followers.

MARATHONS WOULD BE IMPOSSIBLE without the hundreds (and in larger races, thousands) of race volunteers. These folks truly are the unsung heroes of marathons. They distribute race packets and bibs, staff water and aid stations, serve as course officials (and cheerleaders!), and work the start and finish lines. Failure to thank them at every opportunity, let alone verbally abuse them, is considered a major faux pas in the running community.

The same holds true for the people who help you become a better leader. No one, and I mean NO ONE, becomes a great leader without help. These helpers include mentors, coaches, teachers, and role models. And failure to thank them along the way ranks right up (down?) there with failure to thank race volunteers.

But there's one other group you should consistently thank along the way: your followers. Think about it. Just as a marathon would be impossible without the volunteers supporting it, your leadership would be impossible without your followers supporting it.

You might think I'm pointing out the obvious when it comes to thanking the individuals who report to you. Apparently, however, this needs to be explicitly stated. At least according to one Glassdoor survey, which found:

- Only about two-thirds (68%) of surveyed employees said their boss shows them enough appreciation;
- Over half (53%) of the respondents said they would consider staying with their organization longer if their boss showed them more appreciation; and
- A stunning (81%) of respondents said they are motivated to work harder when their boss shows appreciation for their work.[73]

When you read numbers such as these, it's easy to see why renowned executive coach Marshall Goldsmith argues that "thank you" are two of the four most powerful words in a leader's vocabulary (along with "I'm sorry").[74]

Despite these numbers and wise advice from sages, the Center for Creative Leadership has concluded a "gratitude gap" still exists in the modern workplace. For support, they cite research showing that over half of Americans reported saying "thank you" to family members, but only 15% reported saying it in the workplace. Even more disturbing is the finding that over one-third of respondents (35%) said their manager has *NEVER* thanked them![75]

Ways to Show Appreciation

Showing appreciation goes beyond just words. In their book *The 5 Languages of Appreciation in the Workplace*[76], Gary Chapman and Paul White identified the following five types of ways individuals and organizations can show appreciation:

1. *Words of Affirmation:* Yes, saying "thank you" regularly is important for leaders. But JUST saying it doesn't mean a lot unless "Words of Affirmation" is the recipient's preferred language of appreciation. Nor are they the only words leaders should use to show this type of affirmation. Leaders should look for opportunities to praise others for their accomplishments, character/ethics, and positive personality traits (such as optimism, initiative, and perseverance). Depending on the recipient's personality, these words can be spoken or written (handwritten notes or brief emails on which higher levels of management are copied). To put into perspective how important these words are, look no further than Chapman and White's research, which showed that "Words of Affirmation" is the preferred language of appreciation for almost half of all workers (45%).

2. *Quality Time:* In my leadership and organizational workshops, I draw many parallels between effective parenting and effective leadership. And this is one of those comparisons that often resonates deeply with the participants. Yes, we're all adults in the workplace (at least theoretically). But that doesn't mean we don't feel appreciated when an authority figure grants us their time and attention. So, when people need these two valuable resources from you, give them freely. Two key points about this appreciation language: multitasking while interacting with others is *not* quality time, and this language is especially appreciated by younger employees, according to Chapman and White's research.

3. *Acts of Service:* Like "Words of Appreciation" and "Quality Time," the third language of appreciation won't cost you a dime, only time and energy. When things are crazy. When demands on your folks are unreasonable. When tensions are running high. Those are the moments people want to see their leaders "get their hands dirty" and dig into the challenges as enthusiastically and energetically as they are expected to. In fact, nothing screams lack of appreciation

more than leaders who leave their team to solve problems or work long hours on something they think is beneath them. So, look for opportunities to roll up your sleeves and serve others by pitching in when they are feeling overwhelmed.

4. *Tangible Gifts:* The great irony of this language of appreciation is that it's usually the first thing leaders think of when wanting to show appreciation. But Chapman and White's research showed it is the LEAST preferred language of appreciation. In fact, formal rewards and recognition often have a "boomerang effect" by demotivating and even offending people who view the gifts as impersonal or mean-ingless. Leaders using this language should reserve it for those individuals who truly appreciate it. They also must ensure the specific gift is appropriate for that individual. For example, giving someone who hates sports tickets to a local sporting event will result in little more than an eye roll and a sarcastic, "Gee, thanks."

5. *Physical Touch:* As Chapman and White note in their book, this is a controversial and potentially dangerous language of appreci-ation, given the possibility of unwanted and inappropriate touch. Having said that, even after the COVID-19 pandemic, some people welcome firm handshakes, high fives, fist bumps, pats on the back, and even hugs from their peers and leaders. The key is to learn who is comfortable with touch and who is not by observing people's behavior over a period of time. In my experience, it will become obvious which individuals are comfortable with touch and which are not. And even if you think a person will respond to appropriate touch as a form of appreciation, asking them for permission first is always a sound practice.

For a deeper dive into this topic, I encourage you to read *The Five Languages of Appreciation in the Workplace*, which includes the research supporting it and specific "do's" and "don'ts" for each language. For now,

I'll finish this lesson by restating the first lesson of this book: The "point to" leadership is serving others. And part of that service-first mentality involves leaders showing their appreciation for others, especially their followers, for helping them serve effectively.[77]

Great leaders do this. Poor leaders place too much emphasis on themselves, believing they are the main reason for their leadership success.

LESSON 21:
Enjoy the Entire Journey, Not Just the Finish Line.

OVER THE YEARS, I HAVE BEEN FORTUNATE to "pick the brains" of many accomplished marathoners, including Olympic marathoner and run/walk training method guru Jeff Galloway. During one of our conversations, Jeff told me his favorite marathon was also his slowest.

Why?

Because he ran the entire race with his father at what must have felt like a snail's pace to a world-class runner. But the slow pace didn't bother Jeff at all. On the contrary, he was able to enjoy the entire marathon experience, including sharing the accomplishment of his father's first marathon finish, something he couldn't have done if he were running for time.

I've tried to follow Jeff's advice whenever I can. Sure, it's great to push myself hard at races where I'm trying to beat a certain time. But it's also a lot of fun to just run a marathon for the experience, which is why I've stopped during races to pet dogs, dance with spectators, and even down a margarita at a Jimmy Buffett "Parrot Heads" aid station. (Don't judge!)

Many leaders would greatly benefit from heeding Jeff's advice. I've worked with too many individuals who forget that their entire leadership journey should be savored. Instead, they consistently focus only on the "finish line" of goals, objectives, and outcomes.

I'm not saying results aren't important. They are. Nor am I saying the entire journey will always be fun. It won't.

But if you spend all your time focusing on end results, you'll miss much of the joy that is to be experienced during the process. And if *you're* not enjoying the entire journey, chances are your followers aren't either, which means they probably won't want to accompany you on future journeys.

So, how do you enjoy the entire journey?

I've already discussed one of the best ways to learn how to do so: mindfulness. As I mentioned back in Lesson 13, mindfulness is both a state of being and a set of specific skills designed to help individuals be present and live in the moment. Because covering *how* to practice mindfulness is beyond the scope of this book, I've provided great resources on the topic in the *References* section at the end.

However, I can share one simple, yet powerful technique I teach all the leaders I coach, one based on a short story by Russian author Leo Tolstoy.[78]

"The Three Questions"

In Tolstoy's short parable, a king (or emperor, depending on the translation) seeks answers to the three questions he believes are the most important in life:

1. *When* is the most important time?
2. *Who* are the most important people?
3. *What* is the most important thing to do?

Although he offers a great reward to anyone who can answer the questions to his satisfaction and seeks the counsel of many wise people, the king is not satisfied with any of the answers he receives. As a last resort, he decides to visit a hermit who lives on a mountain and is reputed to be a holy man. But this holy man is known to welcome only the poor, shunning the wealthy and powerful. So, the king disguises himself as a peasant, leaves his attendants at the bottom of the mountain, and approaches the recluse alone.

As in most parables, the holy man refuses to answer the disguised king's questions immediately, and the story continues. For brevity's sake (and to encourage you to read the actual story, which is only about the length of one of these lessons), I'll skip the plot twists that occur as the king awaits his answers. But he ultimately does get them:

1. The most important time is now, because the present moment is the only time over which we have control.
2. The most important person is always the person you are with right now, because you may never have dealings with another person in the future.
3. And the most important thing is to make that person you are with happy, because that alone is our life's purpose.

Like the hermit, I ask my leaders to constantly remind themselves of these three answers. And now I'm asking you to do so as well.

Because truly living these three answers will not only help you enjoy the entire journey by keeping you in the present, it will make you a better leader. More importantly, it will make you a better person.

LESSON 22:

Everybody Hits Walls. But Great Marathoners and Great Leaders Learn How to Push Through Them.

IT'S IMPOSSIBLE TO DESCRIBE what "hitting the wall" during a marathon feels like to someone who has never experienced it. But trust me, it is aptly named. One minute you're cruising along, ready to conquer the rest of the course. The next, your legs turn to jelly, your energy level drops to zero, and your mind begs you to stop.

"Hitting the wall" occurs when runners deplete their bodies' stored glycogen (our most readily available and preferred fuel source during exercise). This depletion typically occurs somewhere between miles 16–20, depending on the runner's fitness level and carbohydrate intake during the race. At that point, your body switches over to burning fat as its main fuel source. During this transition, our bodies struggle to maintain physical, mental, and emotional control—hence "hitting the wall." (This is a VERY simplistic summary of what is an extremely complex process in our bodies.)[79]

The bad news is that every runner will encounter this wall during a marathon as their body makes this fuel switch. The good news is two-fold:

1. Effective training prior to the race and appropriate fueling during the race will shorten the transition so much so that a professional runner's wall may last mere seconds; and
2. If you can push through the wall, things usually improve dramatically, and you may even finish stronger than you were prior to hitting the wall.

As a leader, you also will hit many walls in the course of your career. These walls may be at the micro level when someone or something gets in the way of you accomplishing a specific goal or completing a specific project. Or they can occur at the macro level when you find long-term goals or even your entire career path blocked by external forces.

How you respond to these inevitable barriers will go a long way in determining your success as a leader. Because when frustration, anger, despair, and exhaustion begin to wear you down in your leadership role, you have two choices:

1. You keep putting one foot in front of the other and hope it gets better (which it usually does); or
2. You quit.

Unfortunately, too many people choose the latter and give up too easily, both on the marathon course and during their leadership careers. But you don't have to be one of them. You can learn to overcome walls. And the first step in learning how to do so is by adopting the right mindset.

"The Wall Isn't IN Your Way. The Wall IS Your Way."

You want to know what a marathon without the threat of "hitting the wall" is called? A half-marathon, 10K, or 5K. Seriously. What makes running 26.2 miles both challenging and rewarding is the fact that anyone hoping to complete that distance will have to conquer the wall. *The wall IS the marathon.* Runners wishing to avoid the threat of hitting "the wall" need to confine themselves to shorter distances.

Similarly, anyone wishing to avoid walls in their professional careers should probably avoid taking leadership roles. Yes, individual contributors face walls too. But those are more like hurdles in comparison to the walls leaders face. And the higher you climb in an organization, the higher (and harder) those walls become. It is critical that individuals wanting to be great leaders embrace the walls they will hit rather than try to avoid them.

To help the leaders I work with adopt this mindset, I ask them to read and then process with me two wonderful books: Ryan Holiday's *The Obstacle Is the Way* and Angela Duckworth's *Grit*.[80] You should too.

Holiday's book draws on the ancient (but still extremely relevant) teachings of Stoicism, a philosophy born in Greece but refined and widely practiced during the height of the Roman Empire. Specifically, Holiday bases this powerful work on the writings of one of Rome's greatest emperors, Marcus Aurelius, who observed in his timeless classic *Meditations*:

"Our actions may be impeded ... but there can be no impeding our intentions or dispositions. Because we can accommodate and adapt. The mind adapts and converts to its own purposes the obstacle to our acting. *The impediment to action advances action. What stands in the way becomes the way* [Emphasis added]."[81]

Can I get an "Amen!"?

All joking aside, reading Holiday's book and then processing it with a trusted coach or mentor will help you learn "the timeless art of turning trials into triumph" (the book's apt subtitle).

Although Duckworth's methodology and underlying research in her bestseller *Grit* has recently come under fire for lack of replicability, her take on developing your passion and perseverance (a combination she calls "grit") will also help you embrace the walls you'll encounter in your personal and professional lives.

A Final Thought About Walls

My running hero is the legendary Czech runner Emil Zátopek, who remains the only Olympian to win gold medals in the 5K, 10K, and marathon … AT THE SAME OLYMPIAD! (Helsinki in 1952).[82] That amazing feat is why the editors of *Runner's World* magazine named Zápotek the greatest runner of all time in 2013.

So, yes, Emil Zátopek knew a thing or two about running, including "hitting the wall." That's why people should take his following observation to heart: "If you want to run, run a mile. If you want to experience a different life, run a marathon."

With apologies to the legendary runner, I'll wrap up this lesson by paraphrasing his words in the context of leadership:

> *"If you want to accomplish things, be an individual*
> *contributor. If you want to transform lives, including your*
> *own, embrace 'the wall' and become a marathon leader."*

LESSON 23:

Even with Great Preparation, Things Can Go Horribly Wrong—Without Obvious Explanations as to Why.

IF YOU TALK TO ENOUGH MARATHONERS about past race experiences, you'll eventually hear some variation of the following tale:

"I got to the starting line that morning absolutely certain I was going to run a magical race. My training program, nutrition plan, and final race prep were all executed flawlessly. I felt strong, rested, and ready to go. Then I proceeded to run a terrible race … with absolutely no explanation as to why."

On the other hand, I personally have lined up at the start of a marathon wondering how I was ever going to finish 26.2 miles that day because of illness, injury, or poor execution of my training plan. Then I proceeded to run a tremendous race.

These race experiences illustrate the age-old expression: "Humans propose, gods dispose." Please don't get hung up on the religious connotation. It simply means that all the planning in the world does not ensure success.

Leaders too often forget this simple, yet profound, maxim.

They create detailed business cases to help them make difficult decisions. They engage in thorough market/consumer analyses before developing and distributing a product they're absolutely certain will set sales records. They complete comprehensive return on investment (ROI) studies before committing to a major capital expenditure. They develop in-depth three-year strategic plans based on inspirational visions and mission statements.

If any of these endeavors fail, they then conduct after-action reviews (AARs), postmortem meetings, big-data analyses, or cause-and-effect debriefs. Sometimes these activities do result in clear findings and valuable recommendations to avoid similar failures in the future.

But all too often they don't. Because sometimes in life there is no obvious cause and effect.

This is especially true when leading the types of complex living systems I mentioned back in Lesson 3. For while there may indeed be a specific cause or causes of negative effects, those causes may be so seemingly insignificant or so deeply buried in an intricate web of actions and reactions that no amount of analysis will be able to uncover them—a phenomenon known as the "butterfly effect."[83]

The "Butterfly Effect"

In 1961, mathematician and meteorologist Edward Lorenz was running a series of numerical computer models as part of a weather prediction. In one of the models, he abbreviated a value he was entering from 0.506127 to 0.506. This seemingly minor mathematical rounding resulted in a vastly different weather scenario.

Numerous mathematicians and meteorologists throughout history had demonstrated or theorized about the significant impact seemingly minor changes to a weather model's input made in its output. However, Lorenz's work became famous thanks to its creative moniker and oft-repeated (and oft-varied) tagline: "Does a butterfly flapping its wings in Brazil create a tornado in Texas?"

In the six decades since Lorenz's discovery, the "butterfly effect" has become a foundation of both chaos and systems theories. And it is applicable in virtually every organization in any industry in any country.

As organizations have become less like machines (even complicated ones) and more like complex living systems, it's become nearly impossible to identify failures and breakdowns *after* they occur. That's why I taught you "The Five W's and H" as a technique to proactively identify possible failures and breakdowns *before* they happen. Because in complex, nonlinear living systems, that's often the only time you'll be able to demonstrate true cause and effect.

While there's no denying how frustrating this is, there's also no sense in dwelling on it. The reality is that humans cannot possibly predict, control, or sometimes even just understand every variable in any given situation. Great leaders accept this as a natural part of leading in complex, nonlinear living systems, and they simply move on.

That may not be an easy thing for you to accept in the moment. But it's an absolute necessity if you hope to succeed as a marathon leader in the long run.

LESSON 24:

Don't Be So Afraid of Failure That You "Leave Something on the Course."

THE NIGHT BEFORE THE 2004 ARIZONA Rock N' Roll Marathon, I was having dinner in Phoenix with a marathon friend and her husband. As is the case whenever runners get together, the conversation quickly turned from our personal lives to our running lives.

During that discussion, my friend revealed her frustration at being unable to break 3:30:00 in any of her twenty-plus marathons. She had come close a few times and had negative split nearly all her races—in some cases by fifteen minutes or more—but she had never been able to meet her goal. (A negative split is running the second half of a race faster than the first half and is considered the best approach to racing.) I reviewed her training log, which indicated she certainly was capable of setting a sub-3:30:00 PR. But something was keeping her from fulfilling that potential.

Then her husband made a keen observation. He noted she had finished almost every marathon feeling strong and not looking as if she had just run 26.2 miles. This clue, along with her history of ridiculously strong negative splits, provided the answer to her dilemma: She was not pushing herself hard enough during races, particularly during the first half-marathon. In marathon terminology, she was "leaving something on the course."

When I pointed this out to her and asked why she was holding back early in races, she quickly replied with a question: "What happens if I go out too fast, bonk, and can't finish?"

There it was. Right out in the open, alongside our plates of pasta and garlic bread. Her fear of the dreaded "DNF" (Did Not Finish) was the culprit.

I don't think my friend was unique in this fear. Too often, runners allow their fear of failure (a slower-than-hoped-for finish or a DNF) to inhibit their chances for greater success (a new PR or the completion of a longer-distance race). While this approach may be safe, it's certainly not rewarding.

Fear of Failure in Leadership

Fear of failure is not unique to marathoners. In fact, the technique I use to help runners deal with their fears is one I originally developed for executives struggling with their fear of workplace failure.[84]

This self-analysis method is based on numerous human communication and psychology studies, which have concluded that an effective way to deal with fears is by writing about them. You don't have to do so in a formal journal or blog. Any format will do. However, it IS important that you go through the process of actually writing out your thoughts and feelings, because studies show that individuals who take the time to write about their fears are more successful in overcoming them than individuals who only think about them.

Over the next two lessons, I'll introduce you to six questions I'd like you to answer when journaling about your fears of failure. But before I do so, let me make it clear that success with this technique is based on the assumption that your leadership goals are realistic. For as I discussed back in Lesson 7, if your goals are unrealistic, your fear of failing probably *is* justified. Because no mental technique in the world will allow you to perform beyond your current performance levels (in races or in organizations).

Step One: Putting Your Fear of Failure in Perspective

In his novel *Running from Safety*, Richard Bach extolled readers to face their fears head on, challenging them to do their worst. If you don't, Bach argued, the fears will "choke the road to the life you want." And he wisely concluded that failure to lean into your fears allows them to grow well beyond reality, turning a lot of "empty air" into a "jagged hell."[85]

Bach's recommendation to face fears head-on is great advice for your leadership development. If you've set challenging but realistic goals and are following an effective development plan to meet those goals, your fears of failure are probably ungrounded.

To help you put those ungrounded fears in perspective, write down your answers to the following three questions:

1. *Why am I so afraid of failing?*
    You'd be surprised how many times I've asked leaders to answer this question and received nothing more than blank stares in response. These individuals were practically paralyzed by their fears but could offer no immediate reason as to why they were so afraid. However, they couldn't hope to overcome their fears without first understanding *why* they were so afraid. Sometimes, people still couldn't answer this question after spending much time thinking and writing about it, and that in itself was enough to quell their fears. On the other hand, people sometimes uncovered serious and legitimate psychological foundations for their fears. If that occurs during your journaling, don't hesitate to see a licensed therapist, counselor, or psychologist.

2. *What's the worst thing that will happen to me if I do fail?*
    Most of you have probably at least heard of positive visualization, which involves using your imagination to create a detailed mental simulation of a successful interaction. In this case, I'm asking you to perform a NEGATIVE visualization of sorts to put the

possibility of failure in perspective. Specifically, ask yourself the following questions: What's really going to happen if I don't meet my goal? Is my significant other going to leave me? Will my dog refuse to go on walks with such a loser? Will my friends make fun of me? (Okay, that last one probably WILL happen, but what are friends for, right?) Seriously, as Bach alluded to in his novel, our fears too often are self-inflicted "empty air." And a little perspective should help deflate them.

3. *Have other greats failed on the road to their greatest triumphs?*
Answer this question by doing a little homework. It won't be difficult to find magazine articles or entire books about great leaders who have had to overcome crushing failures at some point in their professional careers and/or personal lives. For example, Mark Cuban was fired from numerous jobs and started various businesses that failed before creating the company he ended up selling to Yahoo! for billions.[86] Fred Smith founded FedEx after submitting it as a term project in a class at Yale University. His professor's reaction? "The concept is interesting and well-formed, but in order to earn better than a 'C,' the idea must be feasible." And Steve Jobs didn't become Steve Jobs until Apple fired him, before eventually bringing him back. Years later, Jobs claimed:

"I didn't see it then, but it turned out that **getting fired from Apple was the best thing that could have ever happened to me**. The heaviness of being successful was replaced by the lightness of being a beginner again, less sure about everything. **It freed me** to enter one of the most creative periods of my life."

These, and numerous other stories I could cite, should help you realize that failures are inevitable ... in running, in business, and in life. So, it's not about failing. It's about not letting your fears of failing keep you from succeeding. And, yes, it's also about how you respond when you *do* fail, a topic I'll discuss in Lesson 25.

PART FOUR

Recovering Principles

MOST NOVICE MARATHONERS FOCUS HEAVILY on the first two stages of completing a marathon: training and racing. But experienced marathoners know that the final stage (recovering) might be the most important, even though it's the easiest … at least in principle. The final two lessons will draw comparisons between this critical, but often-overlooked, stage of completing a marathon, and the concept of recovery for leaders and their followers.

In Lesson 25, I'll continue the discussion I started in Lesson 24 by helping you celebrate both your successes *and* your failures. Finally, Lesson 26 will focus on how to avoid burning yourself and others out by encouraging and demonstrating recovery time. This final lesson is critical, because failure to learn and live it will undermine every other lesson in this book.

LESSON 25:
Celebrate Your Successes and Your Failures.

ON SATURDAY, OCTOBER 4, 2008, I stood at the starting line of the St. George Marathon in Utah, looking forward to a race that had been on my bucket list for years. It had the reputation as a fast, downhill course that was perfect to run a Boston Qualifier on. (A Boston Qualifier, or BQ as it's better known, is a fast-enough time to earn a coveted entry into the Boston Marathon.) And because my training program leading up to it had gone well, I was hoping to snag my very own BQ that October morning.

Almost five hours later, after having walked a large portion of the final 10K due to severe leg cramps, dehydration, and hypothermia, my wife had to help me to our car. To this day, it remains one of the most disappointing marathons I've ever run.

But rather than wallow in sorrow, I did what I would have asked one of my marathoners or leaders to do. I celebrated my failure as much as I would have celebrated a successful BQ. Specifically, I treated it as a gift and as a learning experience, one that could teach me many lessons if I just took the time to seek them.

How?

By completing the second half of the activity I introduced in Lesson 24. Because sometimes our fears of failure are legitimate, and we do fail. However, that doesn't mean we can't learn from it. And any learning experience, no matter how painful, should be celebrated.

But before I walk you through how to best celebrate your failures, let me address something I shouldn't have to: celebrating your successes.

Celebrating Your Successes

As I mentioned above, I shouldn't have to remind leaders of this. I mean, what leader WOULDN'T want to celebrate success?

In my experience, far too many.

To be fair, it's not that these leaders don't want to celebrate the successes. It's just that too often they don't take the time and effort to do so. That's an easy trap to fall into if you're not careful, especially when the pace and amount of work is so demanding. But if you *do* fall into this trap, you will lower morale and motivation in your direct reports, teams, departments, and entire organization.

Also, celebrating successes is not purely about boosting morale, motivation, and engagement. Research shows that generating and celebrating wins, even small ones, is one of the most effective ways of increasing individual, team, and overall organizational performance and productivity. And it is absolutely critical to ensuring the success of change initiatives.

In his classic work *Leading Change*,[87] John Kotter argues that true organizational transformation is nearly impossible without first generating and then celebrating short-term wins. Doing so serves two purposes:

1. It boosts morale and builds momentum for supporters of the change, and

2. It simultaneously undermines cynics and resisters of the transformation.

So, make sure you take the time and effort to celebrate your successes. Otherwise, you'll end up "celebrating" a bunch of employee goodbye parties instead. And losing good employees (especially top performers) is not the type of failure you'll feel like celebrating.

Speaking of which …

Celebrating Your Failures

In Lesson 24, I introduced you to Step One of overcoming your fears of failure by contemplating and journaling your answers to three questions:

1. Why am I so afraid of failing?
2. What's the worst thing that will happen to me if I do fail?
3. Have other greats failed on the road to their greatest triumphs?

But what happens if you follow Step One and overcome your fears of failure, only to still fail? Rather than focusing on the negative, focus on what the experience has to teach you for your next attempt.

To begin Step Two of this process, try following the advice of authors Rosamund Stone Zander and Benjamin Zander in their book *The Art of Possibility*. In this highly inspirational work, they note that mistakes and failures are necessary for growth and ultimate success, especially if you handle them appropriately. Benjamin (who is a world-famous symphony conductor) trains his musicians to "lift their arms in the air, smile, and say, 'How fascinating!'" when they make a mistake.[88]

As strange as his advice may sound, I encourage everyone to try it sometime, because it is a great way to perform the attitude adjustment you'll need to dissect the disappointment. But if this technique is a little too "out there" for you, do whatever it takes to put yourself in the right frame of mind before answering the following three questions:

1. *What went wrong?*

    Begin with a detailed analysis of why you didn't succeed. Make sure you write about this in objective, behavioral-based language—not subjective, emotional language. Berating yourself over the failure isn't going to help your next effort. Calmly and intellectually analyzing what went wrong and how you can change future behaviors will. For example, "In retrospect, I should have realized the requested project completion date was unrealistic, given our current resources. Instead of simply agreeing to the client's request, I should have negotiated a later date, which would have avoided a lot of unnecessary stress on my team, as well as produced a satisfied customer." That rational, objective conclusion is much better than, "I really blew it on the Acme project. It's obvious I have no clue how to successfully manage clients or projects. What an idiot!"

2. *How do I feel about it?*

    In answering the previous question, it was important to stay as objective and emotionless as possible so you could rationally dissect what went wrong. For this question, it's critical that you not only admit, but welcome, your emotional response to the failure. Accepting your emotions not only helps you better deal with them, it also allows you to use these emotions as motivation for your next attempt. So, take the time to complete statements such as: "I'm angry about this because ...," "I'm really disappointed about my performance because ...," or "It's so frustrating because ..."

3. *What can I do differently next time?*

    Answering this final question should lay the foundation for behavioral changes. Focus on exactly what you learned from the failure and what you'll do differently to prevent the same thing from happening again. To continue the above example, you might write, "In the future, I will not simply acquiesce to unrealistic client timetables. Instead, I'll carefully design a realistic project plan that will limit the stress my team endures in completing the project and will also result in a satisfied customer. To do so, I will pick my boss's brain about how to both set realistic project deadlines and convince the client that the later deliverable date is preferable for everyone (including them)."

Taking the time to complete this activity will allow you to calmly and intellectually:

- Discover where you went wrong,
- Accept your negative emotions surrounding the disappointment, and
- Identify what behavioral changes you need to make to be successful next time.

A Final Thought

The legendary communication scholar and philosopher Kenneth Burke once famously observed that, "Man [humanity] … is rotten with perfection."[89] He was right. We humans *are* too obsessed with perfection. We live in mortal fear of failure, too often viewing it as a personality flaw instead of a wonderful opportunity to learn and grow.

I hope the questions in Lesson 24 and 25 help you overcome your perfection complex. Because the inability (or unwillingness) to do so will lead to unhappiness, stress, and burnout. The critical step in avoiding this outcome is covered in the final lesson every leader must learn and live.

LESSON 26:
Allow Recovery Time.

IF YOU LIVE AND LEARN THE FIRST 25.2 LESSONS, you'll already be on your way to becoming a much better leader. But to truly become a marathon leader, one built for long-term success, you absolutely must master this final lesson.

For runners, the general rule of thumb for recovery is one day for each mile of a race during which they gave full effort. (Races run at a relaxed pace for fun or as a planned workout for a future targeted race don't count.) This means a runner should not do intense training for at least three days after a 5K race, a week after a 10K race, two weeks after a half-marathon, and about four weeks after a full marathon.

Unfortunately, there's no similar recovery formula for leaders and their teams. That doesn't mean recovery time in the workplace is any less important. It just means we don't have a comparable formula.

But we desperately need one.

Because even before the COVID-19 pandemic hit and made the situation MUCH worse, leaders were burning themselves and their team members out at an alarming rate. In fact, the World Health Organization formally recognized burnout as an "occupational disease" in May 2019.[90]

Leadership and Burnout

Burnout is different from general stress, which all of us experience at times in both our professional and personal lives. Periods of stress ebb and flow, no matter how intense one's job is. Burnout, on the other hand, is a potentially dangerous state brought on by prolonged exposure to stress.

More specifically, it is the inability to perform at a previously successful level due to chronic physical, mental, and emotional exhaustion. A good night's sleep, relaxation techniques, or a day off should decrease your stress. Overcoming burnout, however, might require professional help, extended time away from work, or even a new job.

Just how widespread is burnout among leaders?

DDI, one of the world's largest learning and development organizations, reported the following startling statistics in their *Global Leadership Forecast 2021*:

- 60% of all surveyed leaders said they are "used up" at the end of each day.
- Because of this burnout, 44% of those leaders claimed they are likely to change companies at some future point.
- In the short term, 26% of those who said they are burned out expect to leave their current organization within the next year ... compared to only 6% of those who say they *aren't* burned out.[91]

It's even worse at the executive level.

For example, one study found that senior executives are in performance mode about 85% of the time.[92] In comparison, professional athletes are in performance mode only about 20% of the time! Without adequate recovery, these executives are destined to see a drop in their performance and ultimately burn out.

And it's not solely leaders who burned out.[93] Employees at all levels of an organization are susceptible.

A recent Gallup study found that 23% of employees reported feeling burned out at work very often or always, while an additional 44% reported feeling burned out sometimes.[94] That means approximately two-thirds of all employees are experiencing burnout on the job. Unfortunately, that same survey also found that bad leadership and/or management is a major cause of this burnout, which means it's a vicious cycle of burned-out leaders creating burned-out employees. And that degree of burnout leads to serious consequences.

How serious?

Here are a couple of the profound health effects of burnout mentioned in that Gallup study:

- Employees who are burned out are 63% more likely to a take a sick day.
- Even more chilling, they are 23% more likely to visit the emergency department!

Furthermore, the *Harvard Business Review* estimates that burnout accounts for anywhere from $125 billion to $190 billion in health care spending each year.[95] And in terms of specific maladies, burnout has been shown to increase type 2 diabetes, coronary heart disease, gastrointestinal issues, high cholesterol, and even death for those under the age of forty-five, according to a 2017 study in the journal *PLoS One*.[96]

And that's just the physical toll.

Burnout's toll on our emotional and mental health is even more frightening. That's especially the case since the COVID-19 pandemic forced millions in the United States (and billions worldwide) to work from home, blurring the line between performance and downtime, which has led to a large increase in working hours.

But rather than bog down this final lesson with more statistics about just how bad the emotional and mental states of burned-out workers are right now, I'll end it with suggestions for avoiding burnout. Because the best way to handle it is to avoid it in the first place.

How to Avoid Burnout

As with many topics throughout this book, there is no single "magic formula" to avoid burnout. However, I have found that my coachees who get plenty of the seven types of rest identified by Saundra Dalton-Smith, MD, in her book *Sacred Rest*, seem to avoid burning themselves out:

1. *Physical Rest:* First and foremost, this is getting the appropriate amount of sleep for your individual needs (which Dr. Dalton-Smith calls "Passive Physical Rest"). While everyone's sleep needs are different, studies indicate almost all of us could use more of it. The second type of physical rest, which Dalton-Smith calls "Active," includes any activity that restores the body (yoga, massage therapy, stretching, etc.).

2. *Mental Rest:* Like our bodies, our minds also need rest. Therefore, leaders need to force themselves to give their brains periodic breaks as well. I urge my coachees to use their phone, computer, or smart-watch to schedule short breaks at regular intervals. These breaks can include a brief walk or a healthy snack break (basically any activity that doesn't involve thinking).

3. *Sensory Rest:* Closely related to Mental Rest, this involves taking a break from all of the stimuli that barrage us constantly. That means turning off your phone, computer, television, and any other electronics. It also means, if possible, shutting off the lights for a while. And you might consider purchasing and regularly wearing noise-blocking headphones.

4. *Social Rest:* Even the most extroverted among us need a break from other people. And the more introverted you are, the more alone

time you'll need to carve out for yourself. But this is not just about how much time you spend surrounded by people. It's also about the type of people you surround yourself with. Make a conscious effort to spend time with positive, uplifting people. And also limit or completely cut out the amount of time you spend with individuals who drain you.

5. *Emotional Rest:* Many leaders express frustration at having to maintain a persona that can sometimes feel inauthentic. They feel as if they must say "yes" too often. They believe they must hide their negative emotions. They think they have to give support to everyone around them, in both their professional and personal lives. Taking emotional rest means sometimes saying "no," sometimes allowing yourself to display how you really feel (within reason, of course), or sometimes placing your own needs over those of others.

6. *Creative Rest:* This concept is two-fold. The first is the notion that we can't always be creative. So don't worry if the latest departmental or company blog isn't perfect. (Better yet, let someone else on the team write this one.) And don't feel as if every slide in your deck has to include eye-popping graphics, fun animation, or life-altering content. The second part of this concept involves appreciating the creativity of others. Go to a museum and admire the works of art. Lose yourself in that novel that's been gathering dust on your nightstand. Go for a drive or, better yet, a hike and admire the beauty and creativity of Mother Nature.

7. *Spiritual Rest:* Make sure you feed your spiritual side (however you personally define that concept). That could be practicing mindfulness. It could be reconnecting with a house of worship. It could be volunteering with a local nonprofit. As long as the activity provides meaning outside of your typical day-to-day routine or existence, it should provide Spiritual Rest.[97]

It bears repeating that learning and living the previous 25.2 lessons isn't enough. To be a true marathon leader, you *must* include rest and recovery for yourself and your followers. Failure to do so literally may be a matter of life or death.

Conclusion

I BEGAN THIS BOOK BY ASKING YOU to follow the advice of Lao-Tzu in the *Tao Te Ching* by taking the first step on your journey to becoming a marathon leader. My hope is that the 26.2 lessons you've just read constitute the initial steps of that journey. But learning these lessons was only the beginning. Now you must live them.

That won't always be easy.

Let's face it: Being a successful leader was never a walk in the park. But it's even more challenging in our post-pandemic, hyperpaced, deeply divided world. Leaders are now expected to be diversity and inclusion champions, armchair psychologists/counselors, and international current-events experts … on top of completing their day-to-day tasks!

But as I mentioned in Lesson 6, the very challenge of the leadership journey is what makes it so rewarding. And I hope you've picked up numerous tools, tips, and techniques from these pages that will make that journey easier for you.

To help you along the way, I wanted to share my email address with you: david@marathonleadership.com. Feel free to reach out and let me know which of the lessons resonated with you, and which you're struggling to apply.

Finally, I thought I'd share one other insight from Lao-Tzu's *Tao Te Ching*. I encourage you to think of it as the long-term goal of your leadership journey:

"A leader is best when people barely know he exists, when his work is done, his aim fulfilled, they will say: we did it ourselves."[98]

Acknowledgments

I WANT TO BEGIN BY RECOGNIZING three individuals for whom the word "mentor" doesn't begin to do justice: Dr. Carl Larson, Dr. Michael Spangle, and Dr. Ron Campbell. In your unique ways, each of you have had a profound impact on my professional and personal lives. I would not be the facilitator, coach, and consultant I am today without your collective influence. More importantly, I would not be the man I am today without your collective influence. Thank you from the bottom of my heart.

I also want to thank the thousands of college and university students, professional workshop participants, coachees, and internal client partners I have worked with over the past thirty-plus years. It may sound cliché, but I absolutely have learned as much from you as I hope you've learned from me.

Special thanks to Polly Letofsky at My Word Publishing. Not only did you expertly guide me through every step of the publishing process, you also connected me to two talented partners: Cheryl Jaclin Isaac at CherylIJ Editing and Victoria Wolf of Wolf Design and Marketing. I couldn't have asked for three more talented, easy-to-work-with partners. Thank you all!

Sadly, friend and running legend Ed Craighead (who I mentioned in Lesson 14) passed away at age eighty-two, just a few months before this book's publication. Thank you for your friendship, inspiration, and advice over the years. You already are greatly missed.

Most importantly, I want to thank my family. To my late parents, Audrey and Denny Knapp, you gave me the best upbringing a man could ask for. You were there when I needed you to be. But you were also wise enough to let me train for and run the marathon that is my life my own way. Thank you for that wonderful combination of support and freedom.

To Lauren and Megan, you may not be my flesh and blood, but no man ever loved two daughters more. Thank you for first accepting me into the family and then loving me as if I were your biological father. (Not to mention helping to create our family tradition of completely inappropriate dinner conversations!)

To Jaxon, Mia, Rory, and Brooks, the four of you make my heart so happy! I hope all of you enjoy the time with your Pop Pop as much as he cherishes his time with you. I hope that decades after I'm gone from this Earth, you'll still be smiling at some of the great memories we've made and continue to make.

To Athena, Apollo, Casey, Sunny, and the rest of our four-legged family members, past and present, each of you have left paw prints on my heart. And my life would have been lesser without your unconditional love. If there is an afterlife, I hope my first experience of it is all of you bounding toward me. What a joyous reunion that would be!

And last but certainly NOT least, Kathy …

You are my best friend, my lover, my wife, my training partner, my travel companion, my everything. Thank you for brightening my world every moment of every day. Heart, body, and soul. For eternity …

About the Author

DAVID D. KNAPP, PHD, is the President of Marathon Leadership° in Thornton, Colorado, which specializes in leadership and organizational development. With over 30 years of experience in the corporate boardroom and university classroom, David has worked with hundreds of local, national, and international organizations—including numerous Fortune 100 companies and federal agencies.

David has a PhD in Human Communication Studies from the University of Denver and remains a competitive age-group athlete. He has completed over 100 full marathons and countless other running events and triathlons up to the half-Ironman° distance.

Visit www.marathonleadership.com to learn more about David and his services. If you or your organization are interested in booking David for a keynote presentation, training session, strategic-planning work, or 1:1 coaching, please contact us at sales@marathonleadership.com or kathy@marathonleadership.com.

Endnotes

1 **the journey of a thousand miles begins with a single step:** Tzu, Lao. 2006. *Tao Te Ching.* Translated by Stephen Mitchell. New York: HarperCollins.

2 **Prior to the 1908 London Olympics:** Switzer, Kathrine, and Robinson, Roger. 2006. *26.2 Marathon Stories.* Toronto: Madison Press Books.

3 **Robert K. Greenleaf introduced "Servant-Leadership":** Greenleaf, Robert K. 2008. *The Servant as Leader.* Revised Printing. Atlanta: The Greenleaf Center for Servant Leadership.

4 **after reading Hermann Hesse's *The Journey to the East*:** Hesse, Hermann. 2001. *The Journey to the East.* Translated by Hilda Rosner. London: Picador.

5 **identified 10 fundamental skills of servant-leadership:** Spears, Larry C. 2010. "Character and Servant Leadership: Ten Characteristics of Effective, Caring Leaders." *The Journal of Virtues & Leadership*, 1.1, 25-30.

6 **But that's where the similarities end:** Others have examined the differences between sprinters and marathoners, including Raghunathan, V. 2010. *Don't Sprint the Marathon.* Noida: HarperCollins India.

7 **Figure 2: The Leadership/Management Continuum:** I am not the only author to identify the differences and similarities between leadership and management. Here are three other sources that examine the topic:

Daft, Richard L. 2015. *The Leadership Experience.* Seventh Edition. Boston: Cengage Learning.

Hackman, Michael Z., and Johnson, Craig E. 2018. *Leadership: A Communication Perspective.* Seventh Edition. Long Grove, IL: Waveland Press.

Kouzes, James M., and Posner, Barry Z. 2017. *The Leadership Challenge.* Sixth Edition. Hoboken, NJ: Wiley.

8   **When Lou Gerstner took over as IBM's CEO:** Gerstner, Louis V., Jr. 2002. *Who Says Elephants Can't Dance?* New York: Harper Business.

9   **Although Apple's iPod was dominating:** Isaacson, Walter. 2011. *Steve Jobs.* New York: Simon & Schuster.

10 **In a nutshell, some of us are born with:** Yoke, Mary. 2007. *Personal Fitness Training: Theory & Practice.* Second Edition. Sherman Oaks, CA: Aerobics and Fitness Association of America.

11 **In 2013, a team of researchers led by Dr. Jan-Emmanuel De Neve:** De Neve, Jan-Emmanuel et al. 2013. "Born to Lead? A Twin Design and Genetic Association Study of Leadership Role Occupancy." *Leaders Quarterly*, 24.1: 45-60.

12 **Because IQ is one's ability to learn:** There is a lot of research around the impact of one's IQ and EQ on success, but these are two of my favorite books on the topic:

Bradberry, Travis, and Greaves, Jean. 2009. *Emotional Intelligence 2.0.* San Diego: Talent Smart.

Stein, Steven, and Book, Howard E. 2011. *The EQ Edge: Emotional Intelligence and Your Success.* Third Edition. Mississauga, ON: John Wiley & Sons.

13 **In his book, *Run to Overcome*:** Keflezighi, Meb, and Patrick, Dick. 2010. *Run to Overcome.* Carol Stream, IL: Tyndale.

14 **In the United States, this mechanistic worldview:** McChrystal, Stanley et al. 2015. *Team of Teams: New Rules of Engagement for a Complex World.* New York: Portfolio/Penguin.

15 **Based on the works of:** The literature supporting systems thinking is voluminous. But here are some of the most important in the field:

Meadows, Donella. 2008. *Thinking in Systems: A Primer.* White River Junction, VT: Chelsea Green Publishing.

Österberg, Rolf. 2003. *Corporate Renaissance: Business as an Adventure in Human Development.* New York: Paraview.

Senge, Peter. 1990. *The Fifth Discipline: The Art & Practice of the Learning Organization.* New York: Currency Doubleday.

Van Zyl, Ebben, Campbell, Andrew, and Lues, Liezel, eds. 2017. *Chaos Is a Gift?* Randburg, South Africa: KR Publishing.

Wheatley, Margaret J. 2006. *Leadership and the New Science: Discovering Order in a Chaotic World.* Third Edition. San Francisco: Berrett-Koehler.

16 **Figure 3: Are You Managing a Machine:** Again, there are numerous authors who have examined this topic, including a number of those mentioned in the previous reference, but the following is a personal favorite: Fox, Matthew. 1994. *The Reinvention of Work.* New York: HarperCollins.

I also recommend the following website: The Society for Organizational Learning. www.solonline.org.

17 **For example, one study showed:** I learned about these studies during a running coach certification. But I haven't been able to track down the specific references. Still, I wanted to include them as examples of how important the brain is in running performance.

18 **Sharon L. McDowell-Larsen and her colleagues:** McDowell-Larsen, Sharon, Kearney, Leigh, and Campbell, David. 2002. "Fitness and Leadership: Is There a Relationship? Regular Exercise Correlates with Higher Leadership Ratings in Senior Executives." *Journal of Managerial Psychology,* 17.4: 316-324.

The Center for Creative Leadership has researched and written extensively on this relationship, including "A Leader's Best Bet: Exercise." n.d. Accessed April 25, 2001. www.ccl.org.

19 **This study is not an outlier:** The following are just a few other works on the exercise/leadership connection:

Bartholomaus, Alex P. 2016. *Endurance Executive: A CEO's Perspective on the Marathon of Elite Business Performance.* Washington, DC: People Stretch Publishing.

Matte, Mike. 2010. *Marathon Fit to Lead*. Houston: Willard St. Publishers.

Neck, Christopher P. et al. 2000. "Observations – Fit to Lead: Is Fitness the Key to Effective Executive Leadership?" *Journal of Managerial Psychology*, 15.8: 833-841. www.emerald.com.

Tobin, Timothy J. 2019. *Peak Leadership Fitness: Elevating Your Leadership Game*. Alexandria, VA: Association for Talent Development.

20 **It was a foundation of Jim Loehr and Tony Schwartz's:** Loehr, Jim, and Schwartz, Tony. 2003. *The Power of Full Engagement*. New York: The Free Press.

For more information on these organizations, I suggest checking out their websites:

Johnson & Johnson Human Performance Institute. www.humanperformanceinstitute.com.

The Cooper Institute. www.cooperinstitute.org.

The Energy Project. www.theenergyproject.com.

21 **Heck, one study even showed an increase:** Entis, Laura. September 12, 2014. "Marathon Runners Make Better CEOs, Study Finds." *Entrepreneur*. www.entrepreneur.com.

22 **In fact, Bob Johansen, Distinguished Fellow:** Johansen, Bob. 2012. *Leaders Make the Future: Ten New Leadership Skills for an Uncertain World*. Second Edition. San Francisco: Berrett-Koehler.

23 **For as the Buddha wisely observed:** Buddha Quotes. n.d. *BrainyQuote*. Accessed December 28, 2021. www.brainyquote.com.

24 **Unethical runners have cheated in marathons:** Switzer, Kathrine, and Robinson, Roger. 2006. *26.2 Marathon Stories*. Toronto: Madison Press Books.

25 **These stories of personal failings are why I encourage:** Siggins, Kerry. April 1, 2020. "Why You Should Have a Leadership Credo." *Business & Industry Connections Magazine*. www.bicmagazine.com.

George, Bill. 2015. *Discover Your True North*. Expanded and Updated Edition. Hoboken, NJ: Wiley.

26 **Figure 5: Sample Leadership Credos:** I want to thank all of the leaders I've worked with over the years who have given me permission to anonymously share their individual credos as examples for others. Your generosity has inspired countless others in the development of their individual leadership credos.

27 **And as Hamlet so wisely observed:** Shakespeare, William. 2003. *Hamlet*. Barbara Mowat and Paul Werstine, eds. The Folger Shakespeare Library. New York: Simon & Schuster.

28 **Nothing in the world is worth:** Roosevelt, Theodore. n.d. *Minimalist Quotes*. Accessed December 30, 2021. www.minimalistquotes.com.

29 **A 2015 study conducted by Brandon Hall:** Brandon Hall Group. "State of Leadership Development 2015: The Time to Act is Now." 2015. www.brandon-hall.com.

30 **In a 2018 Developmental Dimensions International:** Development Dimensions International. "Global Leadership Forecast 2018." Accessed April 24, 2020. www.ddiworld.com.

31 **because someone else has already written:** Holiday, Ryan. 2016. *Ego Is the Enemy*. New York: Portfolio/Penguin.

32 **But as my lovely bride can attest:** If you're interested in reading some inspirational books about overcoming adversity, here are two of my favorites: Anderson, Marcus Aurelius. 2018. *The Gift of Adversity*. Monee, IL: Marcus Aurelius Anderson Publications.

Goggins, David. 2018. *Can't Hurt Me*. Carson City, NV: Lioncrest Publishing.

33 **For example, a runner who completes a 10k:** Pierce, Bill, Murr, Scott, and Moss Ray. 2012. *Run Less/Run Faster*. Revised Edition. New York: Rodale.

34 **SMART goals were first introduced:** Doran, George T. 1981. "There's a S.M.A.R.T. Way to Write Management's Goals and Objectives." *Management Review*, 70.11: 35-36.

35 **But the concept really took off:** Drucker, Peter. 2006. *The Practice of Management*. Reissue Edition. New York: Harper Business.

36 **To combat this, Adam Kreek, a gold-medalist:** Kreek, Adam. "CLEAR Strategic Planning – and Why SMART Goals Fail." February 6, 2018. www.kreekspeak.com.

37 **Stretch goals go beyond current capabilities:** Denning, Steve. April 23, 2012. "In Praise of Stretch Goals." *Forbes*. www.forbes.com.

38 **But you have to be careful:** Sitkin, Sim B., Miller, Chet C., and See, Kelly E. January–February 2018. "The Stretch Goal Paradox." *Harvard Business Review*. www.hbr.org.

39 **one of my favorite marathon quotes:** Beck, Kevin. May 20, 2018. "Marathon Training Basics: Introduction." www.lowellrunning.com.

40 **I have a partnership with the Denver Training Group:** Denver Training Group. www.denvertraininggroup.com.

   The Employer's Council. www.employerscouncil.org.

   Center for Creative Leadership. www.ccl.org.

41 **I highly recommend a subscription:** *Harvard Business Review*. www.hbr.org.

42 **As our thirty-third President:** Truman, Harry S. n.d. Quotefancy. Accessed December 30, 2021. www.quotefancy.com.

43 **I belong to the:** Association for Talent Development. www.td.org.

   International Leadership Association. www.theila.org.

   The Greenleaf Center for Servant Leadership. www.greenleaf.org.

   The Society for Organizational Learning. www.solonline.org.

44 **Deena Kastor is arguably the greatest:** Kastor, Deena, and Hamilton, Michelle. 2018. *Let Your Mind Run: A Memoir of Thinking My Way to Victory*. New York: Crown Archetype.

   Melgares, Pat. 2020. *Chasing Excellence: The Remarkable Life and Inspiring Vigilosophy of Coach Joe I. Vigil*. Flagstaff, AZ: Soulstice Publishing.

45 **People often view coaching and mentoring:** Jacobs, Susan. April 27, 2018. "What's the Difference Between Mentoring and Coaching?" Learning Solutions. www.learningsolutionsmag.com.

Reitman, Annabelle, and Benatti, Sylvia. March 26, 2021. "Mentoring vs. Coaching." Association for Talent Development. www.td.org.

Shubhomita, Bose. June 7, 2016. "What is the Difference Between a Mentor and a Coach?" *Small Business Trends.* www.smallbiztrends.com.

46 **These include the Associate Certified Coach:** International Coaching Federation. www.coachingfederation.org.

47 **For example, I use a four-step:** Marathon Leadership. www.marathonleadership.com.

48 **In 1959, social psychologists:** French, John. R. P., Jr., and Raven, Bertram. 1959. "The Bases of Social Power." In Dorwin Cartwright, ed. *Studies in Social Power.* 150-167. Ann Arbor, MI: Institute for Social Research.

49 **Nearly every definition and discussion:** The research and literature on power since French and Raven's initial study is voluminous. Here are some of my favorites:

Cialdini, Robert B. 2021. *Influence: Science and Practice.* Updated and Expanded Edition. New York: Harper Business.

Greene, Robert. 2000. *The 48 Laws of Power.* New York: Penguin Books.

Heimans, Jeremy, and Timms, Henry. 2018. *New Power.* New York: Doubleday.

Hillman, James. 1995. *Kinds of Power: A Guide to its Intelligent Uses.* New York: Doubleday.

Kanter, Rosabeth Moss. July 1979. "Power Failure in Management

Circuits." *Harvard Business Review.* 57, 65. www.hbr.org.

Kotter, John P. 1985. *Power and Influence: Beyond Formal Authority.* New York: The Free Press.

Maxwell, John C. 2005. *The 360 Degree Leader: Developing Your Influence from Anywhere in the Organization.* Nashville: Nelson Business.

Pfeffer, Jeffrey. 2010. *Power: Why Some People Have It – And Others Don't.* New York: HarperCollins.

Trenholm, Sarah. 1989. *Persuasion and Social Influence*. Englewood Cliffs, NJ: Prentice Hall.

Yukl, Gary. 2002. *Leadership in Organizations*. Fifth Edition. Upper Saddle River, NJ: Prentice Hall.

Yukl, Gary, and Falbe, Cecilia M. 1991. "Importance of Different Power Sources in Downward and Lateral Relations." *Journal of Applied Psychology*, 76: 416-423.

Yukl, Gary, Falbe, Cecilia M., and Youn, Joo Young. 1993. "Patterns of Influence Behaviors for Managers." *Group & Organizational Management*, 18: 5-28.

50 **Basically, it is a combination of two:** The Stein and Bradberry books I mention later in the lesson are my favorites. But here are a few other great sources on EQ:

Bar-On, Reuven, and Parker, James D. A. eds. 2000. *The Handbook of Emotional Intelligence*. San Francisco: Jossey-Bass.

Goleman, Daniel. 2006. *Emotional Intelligence: Why It Can Matter More Than IQ*. Tenth Anniversary Edition. New York: Bantam.

Goleman, Daniel. 2007. *Social Intelligence: The New Science of Human Behaviors*. New York: Bantam.

Gottman, John. 1998. *Raising an Emotionally Intelligent Child*. New York: Simon and Schuster.

51 **Don't be fooled by this definition:** Bradberry, Travis, and Greaves, Jean. 2009. *Emotional Intelligence 2.0*. San Diego: TalentSmart.

52 **The top two EQ programs are:** Stein, Steven, and Book, Howard E. 2011. *The EQ Edge: Emotional Intelligence and Your Success*. Third Edition. Mississauga, ON: John Wiley & Sons.

Stein, Steven. 2017. *The EQ Leader*. Hoboken, NJ: John Wiley & Sons.

53 **I developed and began:** Knapp, David D. January/February 2010. "Mind, Body, and Spirit Training Runs." *Oklahoma Sports and Fitness*, 31-33.

54 **I've provided some great resources:** The following provide a great introduction to mindfulness:

Ackerman, Courtney. October 22, 2018. "How to Live in the Moment: 35+ Tools to Be More Present." *Positive Psychology.* www.positivepsychology.com.

Csikszentmihalyi, Mihaly. 2008. *Flow: The Psychology of Optimal Experience.* New York: Harper Perennial.

Dixit, Jay. November 1, 2008. "*The Art of Now: Six Steps to Living in the Moment.*" *Psychology Today.* www.psychologytoday.com.

Kabat-Zinn, Jon. 2016. *Mindfulness for Beginner's: Reclaiming the Present Moment and Your Life.* Louisville, CO: Sounds True Publishing.

Mindful Leader. www.mindfulleader.org.

Dictionary.com, s.v. "mindfulness (*n*)," accessed September 11, 2020. www.dictionary.com.

Dictionary.com, s.v. "mindfulness (*n*)," accessed September 11, 2020. www.apa.org.

Sutton, Jeremy. January 9, 2020. "What Is Mindfulness? Definition, Benefits & Psychology." *Positive Psychology.* www.positivepsychology.com.

Sheldon, Kennon M., Prentice, Mike, and Halusic, Marc. 2015. "The Experiential Incompatibility of Mindfulness and Flow Absorption." *Social Psychological and Personality Science*, 6.3: 276-283.

55 **For example, management guru:** Peters, Tom. n.d. Inspiring Quotes. www.inspiringquotes.us.

56 **And Steve Jobs viewed:** Love, Dylan. October 5, 2011. "The 13 Most Memorable Quotes from Steve Jobs." *Business Insider.* www.businessinsider.com.

57 **A landmark study conducted by Steve Strelsin:** Bodell, Lisa. 2017. "Chief Simplicity Officers: The Next Generation of Leaders." *Leader to Leader*, 85: 18-24. www.onlinelibrary.wiley.com.

58 **Bodell recommends the following:** Bodell, Lisa. 2017. *Why Simple Wins: Escape the Complexity Trap and Get to Work That Matters.* New York: Bibliomotion, Inc.

59 **In fact, authors Tom Schmitt and Arnold Perl:** Schmitt, Tom, and Perl, Arnold. 2007. *Simple Solutions: Harness the Power of Passion and Simplicity to Get Results.* Hoboken, NJ: John Wiley & Sons.

60 **knowledge I'm happy to now pass on to you:** The following are some great resources on listening:

> Bryant, Adam, and Sharer, Kevin. March–April 2021. "Are You Really Listening?" *Harvard Business Review.* www.hbr.org.

> Daimler, Melissa. May 25, 2016. "Listening Is an Overlooked Leadership Tool." *Harvard Business Review.* www.hbr.org.

> Treasure, Julian. 2017. *How to be Heard: Secrets for Powerful Speaking and Listening.* Coral Gables, FL: Mango.

> Treasure, Julian. July 2011. "5 Ways to Listen Better." www.ted.com.

61 **The first key variable is the size:** Ashkenas, Ron. December 2, 2019. "Are You Adapting Your Leadership Strategy as Your Start-Up Grows?" *Harvard Business Review.* www.hbr.org.

> Miner, Nanette. May 26, 2020. "Own a Small or Medium-Sized Business? Here Are Three Ways to Cultivate Employees' Leadership Skills." *Forbes.* www.forbes.com.

> Trammell, Joel. June 22, 2017. "The Differences Between Running a Small Company and a Big One." *Inc.* www.inc.com.

62 **Finally, an individual's level:** Goldsmith, Marshall, and Reiter, Mark. 2007. *What Got You Here Won't Get You There.* New York: Hachette Books.

63 **At the organizational level:** The following are some of my favorite sources on strategic agility:

> Denning, Steve. January 28, 2018. "What Is Strategic Agility?" *Forbes.* www.forbes.com.

> Center for Management & Organization Effectiveness. "Strategic Agility." December 31, 2020. www.cmoe.com.

> Yeung, Arthur, and Ulrich, Dave. 2019. *Reinventing the Organization: How Companies Can Deliver Radically Greater Value in Fast-Changing Markets.* Cambridge, MA: Harvard Business Review Press.

64 **Before leaders can become strategically:** Grant, Adam. 2021. *Think Again.* New York: Viking.

65 **That means you'll need to:** Kotter, John P. 1996. *Leading Change.* Boston: Harvard Business School Press.

66 **This will require you to:** McChrystal, Stanley, and Butrico, Anna. 2021. *Risk: A User's Guide.* New York: Portfolio/Penguin.

67 **Although she is not the only researcher:** Dweck, Carol, S. 2016. *Mindset: The New Psychology of Success.* Updated Edition. New York: Ballantine Books.

Gottfredson, Ryan. 2020. *Success Mindsets: Your Keys to Unlocking Greater Success in Your Life, Work, & Leadership.* New York: Morgan James.

68 **Drafting involves:** Hutchinson, Alex. October 12, 2012. "Does Drafting Help in Running?" *Runner's World.* www.runnersworld.com.

Hutchinson, Alex. June 29, 2020. "Quantifying the Benefits of Drafting for Runners." *Outside.* www.outsideonline.com.

69 **Based on the Contingency Theory of Leadership:** Numerous leadership models are based on this theory. For more details and examples, see the following:

Blanchard, Ken, Zigarmi, Patricia, and Zigarmi, Drea. 2013. *Leadership and the One Minute Manager.* Revised Edition. New York: HarperCollins.

Fiedler, Fred E. 1958. *Leader Attitudes and Group Effectiveness.* Urbana, IL: University of Illinois Press.

Fiedler, Fred E. 1967. *A Theory of Leadership Effectiveness.* New York: McGraw Hill.

Hemphill, J. K., and Coons, A. E. 1957. "Development of the Leader Behavior Description Questionnaire." In Stogdill, Ralph, and Coons, A. E., eds. *Leader Behavior: Its Description and Measurement.* Columbus, OH: Ohio State University, Bureau of Business Records.

Hersey, Paul. 1992. *The Situational Leader.* Escondido, CA: Center for Leadership Studies.

House, Robert J. 1971. "A Path-Goal Theory of Leadership Effectiveness." *Administrative Sciences Quarterly,* 16: 321-338.

Vroom, Victor Harold, and Jago, Arthur G. 1988. *The New Leadership: Managing Participation in Organizations*. Englewood Cliffs, NJ: Prentice Hall.

70 **The 2007 Chicago Marathon:** Davey, Monica. October 8, 2007. "Death, Havoc and Heat Mar Chicago Race." *New York Times*. www.nytimes.com.

71 **If you watch this amazing finish:** "Chicago Marathon 2007! Ivuti + Gharib Fight to the Finish!" October 10, 2007. YouTube. www.youtube.com.

72 **They were the true definition:** Lynch, Jerry, and Scott, Warren. 1999. *Running Within*. Champaign, IL: Human Kinetics.

73 **At least according to one:** Glassdoor. November 13, 2013. "Employers to Retain Half of Their Employees Longer if Bosses Showed Appreciation: Glassdoor Survey." www.glassdoor.com.

74 **It's easy to see why:** Goldsmith, Marshall, and Reiter, Mark. 2007. *What Got You Here Won't Get You There*. New York: Hachette Books.

75 **Despite these numbers:** Center For Creative Leadership. November 18, 2020. "How to Show More Gratitude at Work: Giving Thanks Will Make You a Better Leader." www.ccl.org.

76 **In their book:** Chapman, Gary, and White, Paul. 2019. *The 5 Languages of Appreciation in the Workplace*. Chicago: Northfield Publishing.

77 **And part of that service-first:** Here are a few other great sources on this topic: Conant, Douglas R. November 22, 2017. "10 Powerful Ways to Give Thanks with Your Leadership." ConantLeadership. www.conantleadership.com.

McGovern, Cindy. July 22, 2019. "How a Simple Thank You Can Make You a Better Leader." Thrive Global. www.thriveglobal.com.

O'Flaherty, Shibeal, Sanders, Michael T., and Whillans, Ashley. March 29, 2021.

"Research: A Little Recognition Can Provide a Big Morale Boost." *Harvard Business Review*. www.hbr.org.

78 **a short story by Russian author:** Tolstoy, Leo. 1885. "The Three Questions." www.archive.org.

79 **This is a VERY simplistic summary:** The following sources do a terrific job of explaining what causes "hitting the wall" in great detail:

> Finke, Patti, and Finke, Warren. 2003. *Marathoning: Start to Finish.* Tualatin, OR: wY'east Consulting.

> Finke, Patti, and Finke, Warren. 2009. *RRCA Coaching Certification.* Tualatin, OR: wY'east Consulting.

> Noakes, Tim. 2003. *The Lore of Running.* Fourth Edition. Champaign, IL: Human Kinetics.

80 **I ask them to read and then process:** Duckworth, Angela. 2018. *Grit: The Power of Passion and Perseverance.* New York: Scribner.

> Holiday, Ryan. 2014. *The Obstacle Is the Way.* New York: Portfolio/Penguin.

81 **who observed in his timeless classic:** Aurelius, Marcus. 2003. *Meditations.* Translated by Gregory Hay. New York: Modern Library.

82 **My running hero is the legendary Czech:** Wikipedia. n.d. "Emil Zátopek." Accessed May 6, 2021. www.wikipedia.org.

83 **a phenomenon known as:** Wikipedia. n.d. "Butterfly Effect." Accessed May 8, 2021. www.wikipedia.org.

84 **The technique I use:** Knapp, David D. May/June 2009. "Running from Safety: Overcoming Your Fears of Failure." *Oklahoma Runner.* 18-21.

85 **In his novel, *Running from Safety*:** Bach, Richard. 1994. *Running from Safety.* New York: William Morrow.

86 **For example, Mark Cuban:** Bansal, Annika. n.d. "Ten Famous Entrepreneurs Who Failed in Business Before Becoming Successful." Small Business Sense. Accessed 8/13/2024. www.small-bizsense.com.

87 **In his classic work:** Kotter, John P. 1996. *Leading Change.* Boston: Harvard Business School Press.

88 **try following the advice of authors:** Zander, Rosamund Stone, and Zander, Benjamin. 2002. *The Art of Possibility.* New York: Penguin Books.

89 **The legendary communication scholar:** Burke, Kenneth. 1973. *Language as Symbolic Action: Essays on Life, Literature, and Method.* Oakland: University of California Press.

90 **In fact, the World Health Organization:** World Health Organization, "Burnout an 'Occupational Phenomenon': International Classification of Diseases." May 28, 2019. www.who.int.

91 **DDI, one of the world's:** Development Dimensions International. "Global Leadership Forecast 2018." Accessed July 22, 2024. www.ddiworld.com.

92 **For example, one study:** Astorino, David. August 20, 2019. "Mastering Oscillation: How Peak Performance in Sports and Business are Related." RHR International. www.rhrinternational.com.

93 **And it's not solely leaders:** Gaul, Patty. June 1, 2021. "Leaders Are Burned Out Too." Association for Talent Development. www.td.org.

94 **A recent Gallup study:** Wigert, Ben, and Agrawal, Sangeeta. July 12, 2018. "Employee Burnout, Part 1: The 5 Main Causes." Gallup. www.gallup.com.

95 **burnout accounts for anywhere:** Garton, Eric. April 6, 2017. "Employee Burnout is a Problem with the Company, Not the Person." *Harvard Business Review.* www.hbr.org.

96 **according to a 2017 study:** Salvagioni, Denise Albieri Jodas et al. 2017. "Physical, Psychological, and Occupational Consequences of Job Burnout: A Systemic Review of Prospective Studies." *PloS One.* www.plos.org.

97 **the seven types of rest:** Here are three great resources for Dr. Dalton-Smith's work on the seven types of rest:

Champion, Lindsay. February 1, 2021. "There Are 7 Different Types of Rest. Are You Getting the Right Kind?" *Pure Wow.* www.purewow.com.

Dalton-Smith, Saundra. 2017. *Sacred Rest: Recover Your Life, Renew Your Energy, Restore Your Sanity.* New York: Faith Words.

Dalton-Smith, Saundra. n.d. "There Are 7 Types of Rest. Which Do You Need Most?" *Goop.* Accessed June 28, 2022. www.goop.com.

98 **Finally, I thought I'd share:** Tzu, Lao. 2006. *Tao Te Ching.* Translated by Stephen Mitchell. New York: Harper Collins.

www.ingramcontent.com/pod-product-compliance
Lightning Source LLC
Chambersburg PA
CBHW072143270326
41931CB00010B/1865